2-1-2000

ONE FLEW OVER THE CUCKOO'S NEST

Other Titles in the Greenhaven Press Literary Companion Series:

THE GREENHAVEN PRESS
Literary Companion
TO AMERICAN LITERATURE

READINGS ON

ONE FLEW OVER THE CUCKOO'S NEST

Lawrence Kappel, *Book Editor*

David L. Bender, *Publisher*
Bruno Leone, *Executive Editor*
Bonnie Szumski, *Series Editor*

Greenhaven Press, Inc., San Diego, CA

Every effort has been made to trace the owners of copyrighted material. The articles in this volume may have been edited for content, length, and/or reading level. The titles have been changed to enhance the editorial purpose. Those interested in locating the original source will find the complete citation on the first page of each article.

Library of Congress Cataloging-in-Publication Data

Readings on One flew over the cuckoo's nest /
    Lawrence Kappel, book editor.
        p.   cm. — (The Greenhaven Press literary
    companion to American literature)
        Includes bibliographical references and index.
        ISBN 0-7377-0185-4 (lib. bdg. : alk. paper). —
    ISBN 0-7377-0184-6 (pbk. : alk. paper)
        1. Kesey, Ken. One flew over the cuckoo's nest.
    2. Psychiatric hospital patients in literature.
    3. Mentally ill in literature. I. Kappel, Lawrence.
    II. Series.
    PS3561.E6670538   2000
    813'.54—dc21   98-54650
                                                              CIP

Cover photo: Archive Photos

Copyright © 2000 by Greenhaven Press, Inc.
PO Box 289009
San Diego, CA 92198-9009
Printed in the U.S.A.

"Yes, McMurphy was fictional, inspired by the tragic longing of the real men I worked with on the ward, the sketches of whom, both visual and verbal, came more easily to my hand than anything before or since, and these sketches gradually enclosed for me the outline of the hero they wanted."

—Ken Kesey, "Who Flew Over What?"

CONTENTS

Chapter 1: *One Flew Over the Cuckoo's Nest:* Literary Themes

Fiction's three major elements—plot, characters, and point of view—are well developed in *Cuckoo's Nest*. The novel clearly indicates the relationship among these elements and how each affects the others.

FOREWORD

*"'Tis the good reader that
makes the good book."*

Ralph Waldo Emerson

The story's bare facts are simple: The captain, an old and scarred seafarer, walks with a peg leg made of whale ivory. He relentlessly drives his crew to hunt the world's oceans for the great white whale that crippled him. After a long search, the ship encounters the whale and a fierce battle ensues. Finally the captain drives his harpoon into the whale, but the harpoon line catches the captain about the neck and drags him to his death.

A simple story, a straightforward plot—yet, since the 1851 publication of Herman Melville's *Moby-Dick*, readers and critics have found many meanings in the struggle between Captain Ahab and the whale. To some, the novel is a cautionary tale that depicts how Ahab's obsession with revenge leads to his insanity and death. Others believe that the whale represents the unknowable secrets of the universe and that Ahab is a tragic hero who dares to challenge fate by attempting to discover this knowledge. Perhaps Melville intended Ahab as a criticism of Americans' tendency to become involved in well-intentioned but irrational causes. Or did Melville model Ahab after himself, letting his fictional character express his anger at what he perceived as a cruel and distant god?

Although literary critics disagree over the meaning of *Moby-Dick*, readers do not need to choose one particular interpretation in order to gain an understanding of Melville's novel. Instead, by examining various analyses, they can gain numerous insights into the issues that lie under the surface of the basic plot. Studying the writings of literary critics can also aid readers in making their own assessments of *Moby-Dick* and other literary works and in developing analytical thinking skills.

The Greenhaven Literary Companion Series was created with these goals in mind. Designed for young adults, this unique anthology series provides an engaging and comprehensive introduction to literary analysis and criticism. The essays included in the Literary Companion Series are chosen for their accessibility to a young adult audience and are expertly edited in consideration of both the reading and comprehension levels of this audience. In addition, each essay is introduced by a concise summation that presents the contributing writer's main themes and insights. Every anthology in the Literary Companion Series contains a varied selection of critical essays that cover a wide time span and express diverse views. Wherever possible, primary sources are represented through excerpts from authors' notebooks, letters, and journals and through contemporary criticism.

Each title in the Literary Companion Series pays careful consideration to the historical context of the particular author or literary work. In-depth biographies and detailed chronologies reveal important aspects of authors' lives and emphasize the historical events and social milieu that influenced their writings. To facilitate further research, every anthology includes primary and secondary source bibliographies of articles and/or books selected for their suitability for young adults. These engaging features make the Greenhaven Literary Companion series ideal for introducing students to literary analysis in the classroom or as a library resource for young adults researching the world's great authors and literature.

Exceptional in its focus on young adults, the Greenhaven Literary Companion Series strives to present literary criticism in a compelling and accessible format. Every title in the series is intended to spark readers' interest in leading American and world authors, to help them broaden their understanding of literature, and to encourage them to formulate their own analyses of the literary works that they read. It is the editors' hope that young adult readers will find these anthologies to be true companions in their study of literature.

INTRODUCTION

At the turn of the twenty-first century, Ken Kesey's novel *One Flew Over the Cuckoo's Nest* has a firmly established place in American culture. It has been widely studied in high schools and colleges since it was published in 1962, and more than 8 million copies of the book have been sold. The film adaptation starring Jack Nicholson was one of the most successful movies ever made, winning all five major Oscars in 1975— best picture, best direction, best screenplay, best actor, and best actress. With the availability of feature film videos, millions who never even read the book know the image of Jack Nicholson with a knit watch cap on his head and a basketball under his arm. And they know the story that takes place in the mental hospital ward run by Big Nurse, of the brief stay there of a brawling con man named McMurphy, and the effect of his stay on the patients, especially a Native American called Chief Broom. Along with recognition and acceptance, however, the novel has generated considerable conflict and controversy.

CUCKOO'S NEST AND YOUTH CULTURE

By the mid-1960s, *Cuckoo's Nest* had already become a cultural icon comparable to Jack Kerouac's *On the Road* (1957) and J.D. Salinger's *The Catcher in the Rye* (1951). Like its predecessors, *Cuckoo's Nest* spoke powerfully to and for many late adolescent and young adult readers. The fact that most academic critics dismissed these novels—and many members of the older generation were put off by or did not seem to "get" them—only legitimized the books further in the eyes of the young and intensified their identification with them. And so *Cuckoo's Nest*, like *On the Road* and *The Catcher in the Rye*, was read and reread, embraced as a quasi-scriptural text by adherents of the emerging youth culture.

Kesey's novel proclaimed an attitude of resistance and activism. Some conservatives found this subversive and dangerous while some radicals viewed it as prophetic and inspi-rational. The intense appeal of the book to those on the brink of adulthood, not only in the 1960s but also in all of the decades since, has proved to be one of the universal and en-during qualities of *One Flew Over the Cuckoo's Nest.*

MORE CONTROVERSY

The conservative controversy about the book's apparent en-couragement of rebellion was answered by a liberal contro-versy. Feminists in the early 1970s began to question the rev-olutionary credentials of *Cuckoo's Nest.* They were disturbed by what they considered a negative portrayal of women as oppressors, like Nurse Ratched, or as prostitutes with hearts of gold, like McMurphy's girlfriend, Candy Starr. Critic Leslie Horst clearly expressed this conflict: "Our society has enough derogation of women as it is, and it is distressing to find such a large dose of it so attractively packaged in an oth-erwise wonderful novel."[1]

Further controversy came when author Ken Kesey de-nounced the Jack Nicholson film—its popularity with the general public notwithstanding. While some critics agreed with Kesey, others found the film superior to the novel. A third group found the film and the book equally objection-able. The pattern of controversy in connection with the film version of *Cuckoo's Nest* continued as Kesey sued the pro-ducers and won a small settlement, but it barely attracted no-tice as the film swept on to great success.

NARRATIVE POINT OF VIEW

Even so, many readers of *Cuckoo's Nest* are bothered by the film's inability or unwillingness to provide a cinematic equivalent for the novel's point of view. The narrator of the novel is Chief Broom, a paranoid schizophrenic mental pa-tient who experiences hallucinations and delusions while slowly recovering his sanity. Critics charge that to tell such a psychological story externally and objectively, as the film does, rather than internally and subjectively, as the novel does, is a drastic oversimplification. This unusual and chal-lenging point of view of *Cuckoo's Nest,* however, is only part of its complexity and richness as a work of literature.

The critical essays selected for Greenhaven Press's literary companion to Ken Kesey's *One Flew Over the Cuckoo's Nest* explore that complexity and richness. Each of the essays is introduced by a guide to its key points, which are further identified within each essay through subheadings. Additionally, inserts within selected essays illuminate important ideas and provide supplemental information. An annotated table of contents offers brief previews of the individual essays as well.

A detailed biographical introduction and an overview of the novel's plot and characters are also included for convenient reference. A chronology of key dates in Kesey's life and career provides historical context. Further reading on Kesey and *Cuckoo's Nest* is indicated, and research is facilitated by a bibliography that avoids excessively scholarly and theoretical material. These tools, along with the essays, provide the basis of an enhanced reading of *One Flew Over the Cuckoo's Nest*.

NOTES

1. Leslie Horst, "Bitches, Twitches, and Eunuchs: Sex-Role Failure and Caricature," *Lex et Scientia: The International Journal of Law and Science,* 1977, p. 17.

KEN KESEY: LIFE BEFORE, DURING, AND AFTER AN EXTRAORDINARY INTERLUDE

Thus far, most of Ken Kesey's life has been much like most people's lives. His early years, for example, were somewhat deprived and unstable, as were the lives of many Americans during the Great Depression of the 1930s, when Kesey was born. But as the country prospered after World War II during the late 1940s and 1950s, so did the Kesey family. Ken came into his own as a teenager in a very all-American way that carried through his college years. An outdoorsman and an athlete, he was bright and well liked in high school; he graduated from the state university, married his high school sweetheart, and had kids.

Kesey has spent most of his adult years—between the 1970s and the 1990s—raising dairy cattle in Oregon and writing. His career as an author has had both dry and productive spells during this nearly thirty-year period, which is not surprising since writing has not been his exclusive or even his primary occupation.

AN EXTRAORDINARY INTERLUDE

This description of a relatively ordinary life leaves out only a brief interlude of about eight years (or about one-eighth of his sixty-four years), which falls in between the much longer periods of his typical growing up and typical adulthood. For Kesey, the years 1960–1967 were anything but typical. This interlude begins with his ingestion of the then-unknown drug LSD as a paid volunteer in a hospital medical experiment. It includes the writing and publication of two acclaimed novels, *One Flew Over the Cuckoo's Nest* and *Sometimes a Great Notion*.

During this time Kesey led a flamboyant group of nonconformists called the Merry Pranksters. He and the original contingent of thirteen traveled coast to coast in an old, uniquely painted schoolbus driven by Beat generation legend Neal Cassady. In California they staged public parties featuring drug experiences, psychedelic light shows, and music. These "Acid Tests" became the model for future rock shows. Thus, the Merry Pranksters contributed significantly to the youth culture that would transform mainstream America in the late 1960s and early 1970s.

A BUSY INTERLUDE

During this eight-year interlude, Kesey was arrested twice for marijuana possession, lived in Mexico for eight months as a fugitive from American justice, and spent five months in a California jail after he returned to the United States. Following his incarceration, Kesey returned to Oregon and raised dairy cattle, wrote, and pursued a family life for the next thirty-plus years.

Tom Wolfe's *The Electric Kool-Aid Acid Test* (1968) documented in vivid detail the adventures of the Merry Pranksters on their cross-country journey, the Acid Tests, and Kesey's fugitive experience in Mexico, culminating in an event called "Graduation from LSD" he staged after his return to the United States and subsequent FBI arrest. Wolfe's widely admired landmark work of "New Journalism" (using literary techniques in writing about real events) immortalized this period of Kesey's life in the public eye.

To appreciate Kesey's full life as a real person's experience, we must look not only at those extraordinary eight years—when, among Kesey's other unusual experiences, he wrote *One Flew Over the Cuckoo's Nest*—but also at the many years that preceded and followed them.

GROWING UP OUT WEST

Ken Kesey was born to Geneva and Fred Kesey on September 17, 1935, in La Junta, Colorado. There, his father was struggling to start a creamery and raise a family in a "Low Rent, bottomdog shack," according to Kesey. When World War II broke out, Fred enlisted in the navy and moved his family (which consisted of four members after the birth of Ken's younger brother, Chuck) to Eugene, Oregon. While Fred was at sea, Geneva and the boys moved back to Colorado. When he was stationed near San Francisco, they relocated to the Bay Area. After Fred was discharged from the navy in 1946, the Kesey family finally settled permanently in the Eugene area.

Both sides of the family were farmers and ranchers, but they were also restless wanderers in search of opportunity. Over several generations, they had migrated west to Oregon and Colorado from Tennessee and Arkansas. Having crossed the country, the Keseys and the Smiths (his maternal relatives) identified with rugged individualism and the American West. This cultural heritage would deeply influence Ken Kesey's writing, particularly in the vividly described and distinctively western locales of his novels, and in the creation of heroes of extraordinary grit and determination. When he was a boy, his favorite reading was the pulp magazine cowboy fiction of Zane Grey, after whom he would name his first son.

Ken and Chuck were raised by their father to be vigorous outdoorsmen and competitors. They camped, hunted ducks and deer, and fished for trout and salmon in the forests and streams of the Cascade Mountains. They swam and ran the rapids on inner tubes in the Willamette and McKenzie Rivers in western Oregon. They boxed, wrestled, and raced. These rituals of nature and manhood, and the values derived from them, play a significant role in Kesey's novels (as they do in the novels of other American writers such as Jack London and Ernest Hemingway).

As a boy, Kesey often spent weekends and holidays at his paternal grandfather's farm. There, he listened to his father and grandfather swapping jokes and stories with their friends and relatives. This experience was a direct influence on Kesey's colorful, folksy narrative style, a Western tradition dating back to the tall tales and mining camps of the nineteenth century.

PROSPERITY AND AN ALL-AMERICAN BOYHOOD

During the postwar years, Fred became quite successful in the dairy business. He founded the Eugene Farmers Cooperative and developed it into the biggest dairy operation in the Willamette Valley. The emblems of Fred's success were his suburban home and his private plane. For Ken, this stability and prosperity meant an adolescence that Tom Wolfe characterizes as an expression of postwar American optimism, privilege, and confidence:

> It was very Heaven to be the first wave of the most extraordinary kids in the history of the world . . . to be very Superkids! . . . feeling immune, beyond calamity. One's parents remembered the sloughing common order, War & Depression—but Superkids knew only the emotional surge of the great payoff

when nothing was common any longer—The Life! A glorious place, a glorious age.[1]

Just as the harsher conditions and the numerous moves of his early years had been representative of the 1930s, Kesey's adolescent experience was representative of the 1950s, complete with the imagery of the film *American Graffiti* and its television spin-off, *Happy Days.*

SPORTS AND ACTING

In high school, Kesey's athleticism distinguished him as a football player and a wrestler. But another side of his personality emerged as well—he liked to perform. "That boy could draw a crowd in a desert," his father has said of the young Ken. He learned to put on magic shows, which included ventriloquism and hypnotism. Winning the Best Thespian Award in high school, Kesey was voted most likely to succeed in his class.

While attending the University of Oregon, Kesey majored in speech and communications. He continued performing and won another thespian award. His summers were spent in Hollywood, where he tried to land movie roles. Kesey's athletic activity continued in college as well. He played freshman football, then focused on wrestling, for which he received the Fred Lowe Scholarship as the outstanding collegiate wrestler of the Pacific Northwest in the 174-pound weight class. (After college, he trained for—and just missed making—the U.S. wrestling team for the 1960 Olympics.)

FROM FRATERNITY TO MARRIAGE

For the first three years of college, Kesey had found fraternity life a fittingly all-American vehicle for both his athletic and thespian interests. His fraternity days came to an end, however, when he married Faye Haxby, his high school sweetheart, at the end of their junior year in college. In the more than forty years since, Faye has become an icon of serenity and abiding support as well as a business manager and correspondence secretary for Kesey. She is the mother of three of his children and the stepmother of his fourth and youngest, who was born in Mexico to Carolyn Adams. Kesey's union with Faye has survived and flourished throughout the decades and the changes in his life. After thirty-six years of marriage, he dedicated his third novel, *Sailor Song,* to Faye, describing her as "a deep keel in the raving waves/ a polestar in the dark/ a shipmate."

A NEW AMBITION

By his senior year, Kesey's interests in sports and acting were giving way to a new interest in creative writing. He had written short stories and film scripts in college classes, and his professors were encouraging. He decided to become neither an athlete nor an actor, as earlier considered, but rather a writer.

During the year following college graduation in 1957, while working in Oregon and looking for work in Hollywood, Kesey wrote a novel (which was never published) about college sports called *End of Autumn*. In the act of writing that novel, he seems to have been consciously closing one chapter of his life and opening another. In the fall of 1958 Kesey received a Woodrow Wilson Fellowship and enrolled in the creative writing program at Stanford University, located in the San Francisco Bay Area. In 1959 he received a Wallace Stegner Fellowship and continued his work in Stanford's graduate creative writing program for a second year.

During the last two years of the 1950s, Kesey's life began to shift away from its fairly ordinary pattern. This two-year period would be one of transition to his extraordinary experiences of the 1960s. By moving into Perry Lane, the artistic, bohemian community of Stanford, Kesey was gravitating away from the center of American culture and toward its margin, which, in the sixties, he would help turn into a cutting edge.

"DIAMOND IN THE ROUGH"

When he arrived in Perry Lane in 1958, twenty-three-year-old Kesey had been drunk only once in his life (the night before his wedding with his fraternity brothers) and had never smoked marijuana. The naive all-American young man suddenly counted among his classmates and friends disaffected intellectuals and aspiring artists and writers (including a remarkably large number who would become published and famous). To the sophisticates on Perry Lane, Kesey—with his muscular build, back-country directness, and ambition to write—was a "diamond in the rough," according to Tom Wolfe.

Pulled toward society's fringe, Kesey grew a beard, played the guitar, and sang folk songs. He read Kerouac's *On the Road* and hung out in North Beach, the San Francisco neighborhood associated with Beat movement writers such as Kerouac and Allen Ginsberg. Kesey quit working on *End of Autumn*, the sports novel that had gained him acceptance to

Stanford's graduate creative writing program, and started work on *Zoo*, a transparently autobiographical novel about a rodeo rider's son who is transformed by his Beat experience in North Beach.

THE DOORS OF PERCEPTION

Vic Lovell, a Perry Lane friend and graduate student in psychology, dazzled Kesey with the complexities of Freud and Freudianism's ability to account for human behavior. During Kesey's second year at Stanford, Lovell suggested that he consider, as a way of earning some extra cash, joining him as a paid volunteer in a medical experiment. While earning twenty to seventy-five dollars a session, their job was to ingest experimental drugs, then be examined and questioned by doctors and researchers at the Menlo Park Veterans Administration mental hospital.

Kesey acted on the suggestion. Although he found the clinical atmosphere absurdly inappropriate for the experiment, he was fascinated by the altered perception resulting from these government-sponsored forays into LSD and other psychedelic drugs. Thus began the eight-year interlude in Kesey's life when nothing was ordinary.

For the next few months, he regularly participated in these experiments, and he became especially interested in whether the altered awareness he experienced while on these drugs could be expressed in his writing and used strategically in a novel. Aldous Huxley, the author of *Brave New World* (1932), had experienced the psychedelic drug mescaline and written about it in *The Doors of Perception* (1954). Huxley's title was quoted from *The Marriage of Heaven and Hell* by English mystic poet William Blake: "If the doors of perception were cleansed every thing would appear to man as it is, infinite." Following Huxley's lead, Kesey and his Perry Lane cohorts began to experiment informally on their own with peyote, the cactus plant traditionally used by Native American tribes in religious ceremonies. Then obtainable by mail order, peyote contains the psychedelic drug mescaline.

WORKING IN THE CUCKOO'S NEST

Vic Lovell soon made another suggestion for picking up some extra money: Kesey could get a job as an orderly at the same mental hospital where they had taken part in the drug experiments. Again taking his friend's advice, Kesey figured he would have time to work on his writing during the long stretches between duties on the night shift.

Kesey, however, got distracted by the patients and staff he got to know at the hospital and by the system of administration used to control and "rehabilitate." He began both drawing and writing sketches of his patients.

> I studied inmates as they daily wove intricate and very accurate schizophrenic commentaries of the disaster of their environment, and had found that merely by ingesting a tiny potion I could toss word salad with the nuttiest of them, had discovered that if I plied my consciousness with enough of the proper chemicals it was impossible to preconceive, and when preconception is fenced out, truth is liable to occur.[2]

He dropped *Zoo,* the North Beach novel, and began writing a new novel about the mental hospital.

ENTER CHIEF BROMDEN

Something seemed amiss with the new project. As Kesey wrote in a letter to a friend at the time, "The book I have been doing on the lane is a third person work, but something was lacking; I was not free to impose my perception and bizarre eye on the god-author who is supposed to be viewing the scene."[3]

Then, under the influence of peyote, Kesey conceived Chief Broom, the schizophrenic narrator. According to Kesey, "It was after choking down eight of the little cactus plants that I wrote the first three pages. These pages remained almost completely unchanged through the numerous rewrites the book went through, and from this spring I drew all the passion and perception the narrator spoke with during the ten months' writing that followed."[4] Kesey would later arrange to receive electroshock therapy in order to accurately describe the treatment in the still-untitled novel.

While working on the novel in the fall of 1960, Kesey would read sections of it to Malcolm Cowley's creative writing seminar at Stanford. Cowley, the Viking Press editor who had published Kerouac's *On the Road,* was impressed with Kesey's work:

> His first drafts must have been written at top speed; they were full of typing errors, as if the words had come piling out of a Greyhound bus too fast to have their clothes brushed. . . . He had his visions, but he didn't have the fatal notion of some Beat writers that the first hasty account of a vision was a sacred text not to be tampered with. He revised, he made deletions and additions; he was working with readers in mind. I continued to be excited about Kesey's work as the manuscript

grew longer. . . . A year later I was delighted when the manuscript arrived in the Viking office, this time with a title: *One Flew Over the Cuckoo's Nest.*[5]

Kesey dedicated the novel to Vic Lovell, who had twice enlightened him, first in one direction with Freud and then in another with LSD. Hence, the paradoxical dedication of *Cuckoo's Nest:* "To Vik Lovell/ who told me dragons did not exist,/ then led me to their lairs." This ambivalence accounts for some criticism that notes how Kesey mocks and attacks Freudian categories and therapy as part of the novel's content while using these very Freudian concepts to develop characters like Harding and Billy Bibbit.

To Oregon and Back

Having finished *Cuckoo's Nest* in June 1961, Kesey returned to Oregon to help his brother with his creamery business and begin research for a second novel, this one focused on the logging industry in the Pacific Northwest.

Barely distracted by the publication of *Cuckoo's Nest* and the enthusiastic reviews it received in February 1962, Kesey continued to work on *Notion* through 1963, during which time Perry Lane was torn down. He relocated to a ranch house in La Honda, fifteen miles away, where he finished the novel. It was well over twice as long as *Cuckoo's Nest* and far more complex in style, structure, and vision. When it was finally complete, Kesey recognized what a life-and-death struggle the creative act had been:

> In *Cuckoo's Nest* I had the answer before I started. But with this latest book I didn't have the answer. Therefore, it was a good deal more painful, and cost a lot more sweat. I was struggling with myself as to whether I should continue on or quit. When I speak of quitting, I mean both living and writing. I contemplated suicide—only in the manner in which I toyed with insanity while writing the other book. But there are many forms of suicide.[6]

Indeed, the title of the novel is a haunting allusion to the song "Good Night, Irene" by Huddie Ledbetter (Leadbelly): "Sometimes I live in the country,/ Sometimes I live in the town;/ Sometimes I get a great notion/ To jump into the river and drown."

Recently, as he approached age sixty, Kesey looked back over his entire writing career and said this of *Sometimes a Great Notion:* "It's my best work, and I'll never write anything that good again. It's a question of time spent on it. I worked on

Notion for two years without interruption, exploring symbols and characters and letting the narrative take its own way."[7]

CROSS-COUNTRY JOURNEY

By early 1964, a group of Kesey's friends from both Oregon and Perry Lane had begun to gather around him at his new house in La Honda. To celebrate the publication of *Sometimes a Great Notion* in the summer of 1964 and to visit the World's Fair, Kesey planned to drive to New York with a few of these friends in a station wagon. The plan acquired such momentum that thirteen people, in addition to Kesey himself, wanted to make the trip. To accommodate everyone, he acquired a 1939 International Harvester school bus.

They painted the bus wild colors; they also painted the name "Furthur" on the front and "caution: weird load" on the back. The traveling companions wired it for sound and mounted speakers on top of it so they could serenade their environment with live and recorded music as well as with their voices. They also built atop the bus a platform for observation and performances. They would shoot more than fifty hours of film footage of everything they did and saw on the trip.

The bus's driver would be Neal Cassady, the real-life model for Kerouac's hero Dean Moriarty, whose driving adventures had been made legendary in *On the Road*. Having sought out Kesey after the publication of *Cuckoo's Nest*, Cassady would introduce him to Kerouac when they reached New York for a clumsy but real passing of the baton from one generation to the next. Kesey was in awe:

> Cassady was an elder to me and the other Pranksters. . . . He was literally and figuratively behind the wheel of our bus, driving it the way Charlie Parker worked the saxophone. When he was driving he was improvising an endless monologue about what he was seeing and thinking. . . . He would quote long passages from Proust and Melville from memory, lacing his revelations with passages from the Bible. He was a great teacher, and we all knew it and were affected by him.[8]

Fueling this road trip from coast to coast in the summer of 1964 were mind-altering psychedelic drugs, still perfectly legal and largely unknown to the general public; thus were born the Merry Pranksters.

REAL-LIFE NOVEL

After three and a half years of almost nonstop writing on the two novels, Kesey managed to turn the trip into more than a wild vacation. His challenge this time was to attempt to transcend the artificiality and conventions of fiction by making his real life the medium of his next creation, which he would film. Psychedelic drugs had given Kesey and the Merry Pranksters a sense of the infinite creative potential of human perception and expression. Now they were determined to experience that creative potential as freely as possible. They called themselves, only half kidding, "astronauts of inner space."

Of this new endeavor, Stanford classmate and fellow writer Gurney Norman says, "I think Kesey found a new medium . . . in which life itself is a novel." Robert Stone sums up this extraordinary move in Kesey's writing career:

> Ken saw the revolution coming and felt that he had a social mission. He was going to use the power of his personality to do something special. . . . I knew that he had enormous presence and personality. He really liked coping and leading and acting and had great gifts for all of these things. Before long, it was easy to see that he was moving in a direction that was not purely literary.[9]

ACID TESTS

After the bus trip—news of which spread quickly among the emerging "hippie" culture—the Pranksters returned to La Honda to edit their film. There, they were joined by new members as the use of psychedelic drugs (still perfectly legal) began to spread. The parties at La Honda got so large that the Pranksters staged a few of them in public places with music by the Grateful Dead (then known as the Warlocks), light shows, and showings of footage from the bus trip. These so-called Acid Tests attracted audiences of three hundred to four hundred people and were the model for the rock concerts that have dominated youth culture ever since. Thus, the use of drugs, and the new culture based on it, began to spread on the West Coast.

Through extensive interviews with the Merry Pranksters, author Tom Wolfe recreated their story in pretty much their own terms; *The Electric Kool-Aid Acid Test*, published in 1968, has become the major record and source of information about Kesey and the Pranksters.

LEGAL TROUBLES AND A TURNING POINT

In the meantime, one of Kesey's parties at La Honda was raided by police. He was arrested and convicted of violating marijuana laws. While the case was on appeal, he was arrested again for marijuana possession. This time, facing a stiff jail sentence, he fled to Mexico, where he remained a fugitive from justice for eight months. Several of the Pranksters later joined him in Mexico. Kesey returned to the United States and was arrested in October 1966, two weeks after LSD was declared an illegal substance.

MOTIVES ARE QUESTIONED

With a court date approaching—and now facing the possibility of twelve years in jail for the two marijuana charges and the new charge of flight to avoid prosecution—Kesey was released on bail. On October 31, 1966, he staged a public "Graduation from LSD," where he exhorted the audience to shun drug-taking as an end in itself and to move beyond the now-illegal psychedelics. To some, Kesey was selling out the psychedelic movement for his own legal benefit.

The movement had grown significantly beyond the Pranksters through the Acid Tests and through the publicity surrounding Harvard University's firing of psychology professors Timothy Leary and Richard Alpert, whose psychedelic research was labeled advocacy. Kesey's two trials ended in hung juries, and he was allowed to plead no contest to a reduced charge, resulting in five months served in the San Mateo County Jail in 1967.

Kesey was thirty-two years old when he was released from jail. He would be on probation for the next three years, but the incredible eight-year interlude, which had begun with his ingestion of LSD in a government-run experiment, was over.

News came in February 1968 that Neal Cassady, Kerouac's hero in the forties and fifties and Kesey's in the sixties, had died in Mexico. His death marked an unmistakable turning point. When the Pranksters attended the now-legendary Woodstock rock festival in 1969, Kesey declined to go along; and when they returned, they found a sign in his driveway stating simply but emphatically "No." Kesey was "off the bus," and the Pranksters were no more.

SETTLING DOWN AND RESUMING WRITING

Following the roller-coaster life of the early and midsixties, Kesey, Faye, and their four young children returned to Pleasant Hills, Oregon, in the Eugene area where Kesey grew up. They bought a seventy-five-acre farm, where they have raised dairy cattle ever since. Though a few of the former Pranksters live nearby, most have gone their separate ways. Kesey's children have now grown up, and he and his wife are grandparents.

They have also suffered the most sobering of mature adult sorrows: In 1984 their twenty-year-old son Jed died in a car crash while on his way to compete as a member of the University of Oregon wrestling team.

On his farm in Oregon, Kesey has slowly resumed the writing career he had renounced after *Sometimes a Great Notion,* but the transition has not been easy. He completed his jail journals, but his attempts to develop a novel from them over the next few years were unsuccessful. For three months in 1969 he lived in London, where he tried to start a series of recordings of authors reading from their works for the Beatles' Apple Records, but the project fell through. In 1970 Kesey made a movie for children called *Atlantis Rising,* which was never commercially released. He also tried for several years, without success, to edit the dozens of hours of Prankster film footage into a watchable film. And for a time in the midseventies, Kesey was preoccupied with the filming of *One Flew Over the Cuckoo's Nest.*

KESEY ON FILM

In 1971 Paul Newman directed a film version of *Sometimes A Great Notion* starring himself as Hank Stamper and Henry Fonda as Hank's dad. Kesey was in no way involved in the film, nor was it particularly successful. Unlike the filming of *Notion,* however, the situation was just the opposite when director Milos Forman filmed *Cuckoo's Nest* in 1975.

Kesey was involved this time, but in a negative way: He quarreled with the producers, sued them, and refused to see the film. Despite this controversy, the film was a huge success. And Kesey, the author of the original book, got a minuscule eighteen thousand dollars for the movie rights he sold to Kirk Douglas in 1962, another ten thousand dollars for the screenplay he wrote (and the producers rejected), and a small settlement that covered his revisions and compensated him for the unauthorized use of his name.

According to Kesey, "They wanted me to do it a certain way, leaving out the narrative thread of Chief's perspective and making Big Nurse the center of evil." [10] Kesey offered a remarkable anecdote about an old white-haired woman who approached him and asked if he remembered her:

> "Lois . . . Lois Learned, Big Nurse," and I thought, "Oh, my God."
> . . . This was the nurse on the ward I worked on at the Menlo Park hospital. . . . I felt there was a lesson in it, the same one I had tried to teach Hollywood. She's not the villain. She might be the minion of the villain, but she's really just a big old tough ex-Army nurse who is trying to do the best she can, according to the rules

that she has been given. She worked for the villain and believed in the villain, but she ain't the villain.[11]

Ironically, many film critics praised actress Louise Fletcher for humanizing Nurse Ratched, whom they considered a monster in the book—the exact opposite of Kesey's point. But it was not only the film's treatment of Big Nurse that displeased Kesey, who would have preferred Gene Hackman to Jack Nicholson in the lead role.

"Tarnished Galahad"

For almost three decades following the publication of *Sometimes a Great Notion* in 1964, no great literary works came from Kesey. He has called this period "the comedown years—my gonzo time."[12] *Kesey's Garage Sale* (1973) admitted in its title that it was no more than what one critic called "a collection of rusty, dusty odds and ends, going cheap."[13]

It did, however, include three fascinating documents relevant to *Cuckoo's Nest*. One was "People on the Ward," a letter written by Kesey to his friend Ken Babbs about the patients he got to know while working in the mental hospital who were models for his "Chronic" characters. The second is a series of drawings Kesey made of these men as well as the original major characters he was creating, McMurphy and Chief Broom. The third is an essay called "Who Flew Over What?" in which he takes a fresh look at his novel. In the essay, Kesey has acquired a new humility about his accomplishment, realizing that the work chose him more than he chose the work. It occurred to him that Chief Broom was not his creation at all; a voice had told Kesey to chose him as a medium: "It is not something I set out to do. It's as though all the angels got together and said, 'Okay, here's the message that America desperately needs. Now, let's pick him to do it.'"[14]

Reviewing in 1986 the nearly twenty years that had passed since the remarkable role he had played in the 1960s, Kesey published *Demon Box*, a collection of his writings that tries to come to terms with the sixties. *Demon Box* is Kesey's term for the fragments of plots and ideas he is trying to weave together and coax to life at any given time. As its epigraph, he selected a poem he had written as a fugitive in Mexico, which reads in part,

Down to five pesos from five thousand dollars
Down to the dregs from the lip-smacking foam
Down to a dopefiend from a prizewinning scholar
Down to the bush from a civilized home.

What people once called a promising talent
What used to be known as an upstanding lad
Now hounded and hunted by the law of two countries
And judged to be only a tarnished Galahad.

JOURNALISM AND EXPERIMENTAL FICTION

This new collection, with its self-effacing epigraph, represented more than just "a tarnished Galahad." The fits and starts of the late 1960s and early 1970s in Kesey's writing career were beginning to be replaced by more sustained writing in a wide variety of genres.

In the 1970s and 1980s, for example, Kesey did some traveling on journalistic assignments: to Egypt to write about the pyramids for *Rolling Stone* in 1974–1975, and to China to cover the Beijing Marathon for *Running* magazine in 1981–1982. These pieces were collected in *Demon Box*.

Also in *Demon Box*, Kesey looked wistfully back to Neal Cassady and John Lennon, departed heroes of the sixties, in two of the collection's most notable pieces. Of particular interest to *Cuckoo's Nest* fans is a piece of autobiographical fiction called "The Demon Box: An Essay," in which he discusses the making of the film. The character he uses to represent himself in the autobiographical short stories is called Devlin Deboree (pronounced "debris"), the thinly disguised name emphasizing the unrealized and incomplete quality of this work. Both the Cassady piece ("The Day After Superman Died") and the title piece are cast in a very interesting form somewhere between autobiographical fiction and the personal essay.

Kesey's ventures in experimental fiction did not stop there, though. He conceived a stream-of-consciousness narrative to be published in seven annual installments called *Seven Prayers by Grandma Whittier*. The main character is modeled on Kesey's own Grandma Smith, who told him stories when he was a boy and whom he considers a significant influence on his narrative style. Six chapters (or prayers) were published between 1974 and 1981 in a magazine created by Kesey and Ken Babbs called *Spit in the Ocean*, which published poems, short stories, and essays.

During the 1987–1988 school year, Kesey taught a creative writing course at the University of Oregon, Eugene, in which he and thirteen students wrote and published a collaborative novel, *Caverns* (1989), under the pseudonym O.U. Levon (or Novel U. of O. backwards). In addition, Kesey has published two stories for children, *Little Tricker the Squirrel Meets Big Double the Bear* (1990) and *The Sea Lion* (1991).

FINALLY ANOTHER NOVEL

Gaining momentum from this variety of smaller projects, Kesey finally sank his teeth into a new novel in the early 1980s—the first time in almost twenty years. True to his Western roots, Kesey set the novel in Alaska in a little fishing village encroached upon by a film crew using it as a shooting location. His son Jed's death in 1984 created a major interruption, but Kesey resumed, completed, and published the Alaska novel in 1992 under the title *Sailor Song.* Being able to finish it—ten years after he had started it—was a significant and gratifying accomplishment for Kesey.

As the 1990s began, Viking Press seemed to be gearing up for a major Kesey revival. A new book of photographs and inside accounts of the Prankster years, called *On the Bus,* and Kesey's screenplay about Neal Cassady and the bus, *The Furthur Inquiry* (which had turned up after having been lost for twelve years), were both published in 1990 as if to alert the world again to Kesey in time for *Sailor Song.* But after a twenty-eight-year wait, the new novel got mixed reviews. Some reviewers found it worthy of comparison with Kesey's novels of the 1960s, but in the 1990s it was just another novel liked by some and disliked by others.

Kesey, however, went right on—finishing and publishing his collaboration with Ken Babbs, *Last Go Round* (1994). He continued giving readings of his children's stories at schools and hospitals as well, and he performed his new play, *Twister,* during 1994–1995.

In September 1997, at age sixty-two, Kesey suffered a mild stroke, but he has recovered and continues to write.

KESEY AS A PARADOX

Articles on Kesey during the more than thirty years since the days of the Merry Pranksters in the midsixties differ widely as to how much he has changed since then. A story from *People* magazine in 1976 includes folksy photos of Kesey and Faye cheering at a high school wrestling tournament, fixing the kitchen plumbing, helping a daughter with her homework, and coaching their sons in wrestling. Yet another article from *Saturday Review* in 1983 emphasizes the Day-Glo colors that adorn his farmhouse, the silver-and-blue star emblazoned on its exterior, and the stereo speakers mounted in the trees on his property, all of which seem like throw-backs to La Honda and the days of the Merry Pranksters.

On the one hand, when the school board in Idaho Falls, Idaho, banned *Cuckoo's Nest* from the public schools in 1978 for "profane and vulgar language," Kesey implicitly assented by offering lectures on the value of teaching Shakespeare and the Bible in high school. On the other hand, Kesey has not completely given up psychedelic drugs and still uses them occasionally for spiritual investigation; however, he no longer recommends LSD as a tool for writing.

CARRYING ON

The postsixties part of Ken Kesey's life has been a complex process of assimilating the significance of those extraordinary experiences of the sixties—including the writing of *One Flew Over the Cuckoo's Nest*—and discriminating between mere excess and truly liberated perception and expression. To choose between affirming or denying those years, between nostalgia and self-recrimination, is too simplistic. Kesey has risen to the challenge of carrying on his life and his career as a writer without exploiting or ignoring the experiences of these few remarkable years. Instead, he has absorbed, sifted, revised, and moved on in a way that has defined his maturity.

NOTES

1. Tom Wolfe, *The Electric Kool-Aid Acid Test.* New York: Farrar, Straus & Giroux, 1968, pp. 34–35.
2. Quoted in John Clark Pratt, ed., One Flew Over the Cuckoo's Nest: *Text and Criticism.* 1973. Reprint, New York: Viking, 1996, p. xv.
3. Quoted in Pratt, One Flew Over the Cuckoo's Nest: *Text and Criticism,* p. 337.
4. "Who Flew Over What?" quoted in Pratt, One Flew Over the Cuckoo's Nest: *Text and Criticism,* p. 35.
5. "Ken Kesey at Stanford," *Northwest Review,* 1977, p. 3.
6. Quoted in Paul Perry and Ken Babbs, *On the Bus: The Complete Guide to the Legendary Trip of Ken Kesey and the Merry Pranksters and the Birth of the Counterculture.* New York: Thunder's Mouth, 1990, p. 44.
7. Quoted in "Ken Kesey: The Art of Fiction," *Paris Review,* Spring 1994, p. 82.
8. Quoted in "Ken Kesey," *Paris Review,* p. 67.
9. Quoted in Perry and Babbs, *On the Bus,* pp. 35–36.

10. Quoted in "Ken Kesey," *Paris Review*, p. 79.
11. Quoted in "Ken Kesey," *Paris Review*, p. 77.
12. Quoted in "Ken Kesey," *Paris Review*, p. 89.
13. Peter O. Whitmer, "Ken Kesey's Search for the American Frontier," *Saturday Review*, May/June 1983, p. 26.
14. Quoted in Whitmer, p. 27.

PLOT AND CHARACTERS

In *The Electric Kool-Aid Acid Test,* author Tom Wolfe aptly sums up the basic plot of *One Flew Over the Cuckoo's Nest:*

> [McMurphy] is a big healthy animal, but he decides to fake insanity in order to get out of a short jail stretch he is serving on a work farm and into what he figures will be the soft life of a state mental hospital. He comes onto the ward with his tight reddish-blond curls tumbling out from under his cap, cracking jokes and trying to get some action going among these deadasses in the loony bin. They can't resist the guy. They suddenly want to *do* things. The tyrant who runs the place, Big Nurse, hates him for weakening . . . Control, and the System. . . . Finally, Big Nurse is driven to play her trump card and finish off McMurphy by having him lobotomized. But this crucifixion inspires an Indian patient, a schizoid called Chief Broom, to rise up and break out of the hospital and go sane: namely, run like hell for open country.[1]

THE HERO, THE VILLAIN, AND THE NARRATOR

Kesey leaves no ambiguity about McMurphy's being the hero and Big Nurse's being the villain. In this sense, the characters are like cartoons and the novel is simplistic and much like a comic book. However, the ultimate victory of McMurphy's philosophy over the nurse's is somewhat ambiguous because it costs him his life.

But it is the novel's narrator, Chief Bromden, who is its most important and complex character. His paranoid schizophrenic perception includes hallucinations and obsessive fears, which require readers to distinguish between his fantasies and his reality. Beyond that, these hallucinations and fantasies—such as "the fog" and "the Combine"—are significant on a higher level of meaning than the literal, as metaphors and symbols. They indicate Bromden's perception as delusions but also as poetic insight and artistic expression.

Chief Broom is important not only because he is the one telling the story but also because of the way his character changes and develops in the course of the novel—from a frightened man who pretends to be deaf and dumb to one who takes responsibility for his own freedom. This change is a complex process in which McMurphy and Big Nurse are only agents, or reference points (hero and villain), in Bromden's subjective awareness. By the end of the novel, he is able to take the life of his friend and savior, McMurphy, in an act of anguish, courage, and love. The changes he undergoes are a coherent journey to recovered sanity and humanity. In this, he represents all of the inmates, or at least their potential; hence his importance as the novel's central character.

THE NOVEL'S STRUCTURE

Kesey structured this medium-length novel in four parts. While part 1 takes up almost half of the book's total length, parts 2, 3, and 4 (of roughly equal length) make up the second half of the book. This disproportion reflects the relatively leisurely pace of part 1 and the quickening tempo and intensification of dramatic action once the essential elements of character and theme have been established and set in motion. The last part alone, for example, contains more than half of the book's intensely dramatic and significant scenes because the narrative momentum has become so intense as the novel reaches its conclusion. Kesey's effective crafting of this momentum is part of what makes *Cuckoo's Nest* compelling.

Each of the novel's four parts concludes with its own dramatic and decisive battle in the ongoing conflict between McMurphy and Nurse Ratched.

PART 1: MAKING A BET

Chief Broom offers a brief introductory glimpse of a typical morning in his life as a frightened, institutionalized schizophrenic pretending to be deaf and dumb. Then McMurphy arrives and meets the patients, twenty "Acutes" who are usually younger and have potential for rehabilitation and twenty "Chronics" who are simply being warehoused. McMurphy stirs things up from the start. He wastes no time in sizing up the ward and the nurse who runs it and offering his frank opinions on both. After participating in a group therapy session in which Nurse Ratched singled out individuals, including him, and coldly discussed their "situation," McMurphy offers the inmates his thought that the supposedly constructive therapy he has just witnessed is nothing more than a "pecking party" at which the men destroy each other at Nurse Ratched's instigation. She, according to McMurphy's analysis, is an emasculator, a "ball-cutter."

Bitterly agreeing with him, inmate Harding laments that they are too afraid of Ratched to do anything about it because of her authority to prescribe "treatments." These treatments include electroshock and even lobotomy, which, as the patients well know, constitutes punishment more than therapy. The inmates' nascent interest in justice, and in their own welfare, prompts McMurphy to bet them five dollars each that in a week's time he can make Big Nurse lose her dignity and control. He would shatter her hard exterior and expose her as a human being.

WINNING THE BET

The dramatic conclusion of part 1 involves a World Series game on television, which was scheduled to be aired at a time other than the hospital's regular television-viewing hours. Big Nurse is adamant that the routine be strictly enforced. Wanting nothing more than to enjoy a good baseball game, McMurphy generates enough interest among the inmates to request a vote on the question. After a tense showdown between McMurphy and Big Nurse—during which he frantically campaigns for votes and she grows even more rigid and stubborn in her refusal to back down—Big Nurse counts the Chronics, who are completely unaware of the proceedings, as "no" votes and declares the motion dead.

Just as she is adjourning the meeting, however, McMurphy persuades Chief Bromden to cast the deciding "yes" vote. He triumphantly turns on the television. But McMurphy's victory is short-lived; Big Nurse counters by cutting off the television's electricity. Her victory, though, is even more brief. In complete defiance of her authority, McMurphy remains in front of the blank television screen and pretends to watch the World Series. As other inmates catch on to his game, they join in—and Big Nurse loses both her control of the men and her composure. McMurphy has won his bet.

PART 2: CHANGES OF HEART

As a result of his defiant vote cast at McMurphy's instigation, Chief feels empowered. His association with McMurphy has made him less afraid of Big Nurse and more inclined to venture farther away from his safe "fog" of deafness, dumbness, and invisibility. Early in part 2, he looks through the window at night and discovers that he recognizes and genuinely appreciates the natural environment for the first time in years. He reflects on his childhood and recalls fishing and hiking on tribal land. Observing a dog sniffing the ground and a flock of geese flying in the moonlight, Chief feels himself coming alive.

As things are looking brighter for Chief Bromden, however, they are growing darker for McMurphy. Beginning with part 2, Big Nurse makes an ominous change in her strategy. Whereas in part 1 she had recommended that McMurphy be transferred to "Disturbed," she now wants to keep him on her ward to teach him a lesson.

Coinciding with this change in strategy, McMurphy learns that because he is legally committed to the mental hospital, he cannot be released without Big Nurse's approval. Her recommendation is required even if he breaks no rules and avoids punitive treatment. McMurphy's behavior changes immediately and radically.

Gone is the uncooperative, mocking rabble-rouser; gone is the inmates' fearless leader. McMurphy no longer backs them in their new confidence, which was inspired by him. He refuses to support his fellow inmate Cheswick in his appeal to end cigarette rationing. In despair, Cheswick commits suicide by drowning himself in the pool. Big Nurse is winning.

ANOTHER REVERSAL

A single piece of information proves significant in altering McMurphy's behavior yet again. He is stunned when he discovers that while he is legally committed to the mental institution, most of the other men are not. He has assumed all along that they, too, were captives against their will. McMurphy realizes just how desperately they need help when Harding tells him that they have it in their power to simply walk out of the hospital but are too afraid of Big Nurse, of the outside world, of *everything*.

Now McMurphy decides to act on their behalf, not to win a bet for himself but for the men's own sake, even when it represents a sacrifice of himself. McMurphy may have been a selfish con man when he arrived in part 1, but he is fundamentally changing in that he now is moved, perhaps for the first time, to make others more important than himself.

Just as the World Series incident marked the climax of the first part of *Cuckoo's Nest,* a similarly dramatic incident marks the end of the second. When the issue of cigarette rationing arises again, Big Nurse remains a rigid disciplinarian, despite the cruel fate of Cheswick. Bursting with rage that has been bottled up throughout his period of good behavior, McMurphy smashes the glass of the nurses station with a clenched fist and takes his cigarettes right in front of Big Nurse, as if in memory of Cheswick. "He was the logger again, the swaggering gambler, the big redheaded brawling Irishman, the cowboy out of the TV set walking down the middle of the street to meet a dare," Chief Bromden thinks. The inmates are inspired anew.

PART 3: CHIEF SPEAKS

As Chief tackles his demons and his recovery continues into part 3, he recalls how his Native American father was pressured by the federal government and his white wife (Chief's mother) to allow the building of a hydroelectric dam on the river in tribal territory. When McMurphy gives him a piece of gum as he is pondering this, Chief impulsively says "thank you" and breaks out of his silence. With this single act, he recovers a significant part of his humanity.

Chief tries out his new power of speech by telling McMurphy about his father, Tee Ah Millatoona, an Indian chief who was emasculated and demoralized by his white wife. He was also beaten by the loss of his land and way of life to the American government, and he began drinking to drown his problems. McMurphy is the first person with whom Chief has spoken in years, and a bond is formed between the two men. McMurphy convinces Chief to go on an impending fishing trip that he is planning.

THE FISHING TRIP

The fishing trip is one of the highlights in *Cuckoo's Nest*. With McMurphy in charge, the men eat up the adventure of the outdoors as they go out to sea, battle the elements, catch fish, and drink beer. Joining them on the excursion is McMurphy's lady friend, the pretty blond prostitute Candy Starr, in whose presence the patients recover a feeling of manhood. The childlike and stuttering inmate Billy Bibbit is powerfully attracted to Starr.

On the return trip to the hospital, they stop in the neighborhood where McMurphy grew up; and as the men listen eagerly, he regales them with the story of his sexual initiation. He is giving his life to them: "His relaxed, good-natured voice doled out his life for us to live, a rollicking past full of kid fun and drinking buddies and loving women and barroom battles over meager honors—for all of us to dream ourselves into," observes Chief. As an antidote to Big Nurse's regimen of isolation, humiliation, and control, the men get a taste of elemental outdoor freedom, companionship, laughter, and self-esteem.

Nearing the hospital, Chief notices that McMurphy is exhausted; as the patients are gaining new life, he seems to be losing his. Yet the fishing trip that is the finale of part 3 is a sustained act in defiance of Big Nurse—and a dramatic victory for McMurphy and the patients.

PART 4: A FIGHT, A PUNISHMENT, AND A PARTY

The fourth and final part of the novel contains not one or two climactic scenes, like the other parts, but eight of them, as McMurphy and Big Nurse trade blows in a series of extreme and decisive actions.

McMurphy defends a fellow inmate when the staff attempts to give him an unwanted enema. With his fists, McMurphy fights two orderlies at once. Like Tonto helping the Lone Ranger, Chief joins in the fray to even up the sides. And though they are heartily congratulated by the other inmates upon their victory, McMurphy and Chief are promptly sent by Big Nurse for electroshock therapy.

Like never before, Chief is able to resist the effect of oblivion ("the fog") that results from electroshock. Reconnecting with old memories, Chief focuses on a nursery rhyme he learned from his grandmother, including the verse that is the source of the novel's title: "Three geese inna flock . . . one flew east, one flew west, one flew over the cuckoo's nest. . . . O-U-T spells out . . . goose swoops down and plucks *you* out." Indeed, realizes Chief, McMurphy is the goose swooping down and liberating these cuckoos (men) from the nest (madhouse). After the shock treatment, Chief is able to clear his head: "I . . . knew this time I had them beat."

McMurphy emerges from his shock treatment somewhat haggard but all the more determined to beat Big Nurse, and the system she represents, by self-destructively crushing himself into them if necessary. Aggressively pursuing his agenda of freeing himself and the others, he stages an elaborate and drunken party right there in the ward, with the cooperation of a night attendant bribed with alcohol. In total violation of every known hospital rule, he arranges for Candy Starr to bring fellow prostitute Sandy as well as wine and vodka, and the men party with wild abandon. He also arranges for the sexual initiation of Billy Bibbit, who was so smitten with Starr on the fishing trip. Meanwhile, McMurphy

has concocted a scheme to break out of the hospital by daybreak, after one last fling with the inmates. Chief is to ac-
company him.

Discovery, Suicide, and Assault

In a dramatic morning-after discovery, Nurse Ratched finds
her tightly run operation in shambles. Drunken and hung-
over men are sprawled across the floor, furniture is strewn
about in disarray, empty alcohol bottles litter the ward.
Bleary-eyed McMurphy has neglected to escape after the
party as planned, though his commitment to the men at this
point would not have allowed it in any case. Inspecting the
scene in silence, Big Nurse finds a naked Bibbit in the arms
of an equally naked Starr. Enraged, she shames and terror-
izes him with threats of telling his mother, which drives him
to suicide.

Responding to Bibbit's death, McMurphy takes the ultimate step. He physically attacks Nurse Ratched, ripping her
uniform and exposing her breasts—her womanhood and humanity—and then choking her. As he had first noticed in
McMurphy's exhaustion at the end of the fishing trip, Chief
recognizes that in attacking Big Nurse, McMurphy is playing
a role for the sake of the inmates and sacrificing himself for
them:

> We couldn't stop him because we were the ones making him
> do it. It wasn't the nurse that was forcing him, it was our need
> that was making him push himself slowly up from sitting, his
> big hands driving down on the leather chair arms, pushing
> him up, rising and standing like one of those moving-picture
> zombies, obeying orders beamed at him from forty masters. It
> was us that had been making him go on for weeks.

After witnessing and sharing with impunity McMurphy's
crime—his fearless demonstration that Big Nurse is only human—five of the patients who are not committed by the state
summon the courage to walk out of the mental institution
voluntarily, and six more are transferred elsewhere. Big
Nurse's power over the men has been broken.

Lobotomy, Love, and Freedom

Because of the attack, McMurphy himself is totally vulnerable. Big Nurse's revenge on him is nothing less than lobotomy. Chief is sickened when he sees McMurphy—or the limp
body of the man who was formerly McMurphy—as he is
wheeled back into the ward afterward. It takes Chief little
time to realize that there is only one way to preserve his

friend's dignity and prevent his being a trophy for Big Nurse: a mercy killing that is a blow against Big Nurse and an act of love for McMurphy. After suffocating him, Chief, in a fitting tribute to McMurphy, tears the control panel out of the floor, smashes a window with it, and escapes. McMurphy's martyrdom has not been in vain.

NOTES

1. Tom Wolfe, *The Electric Kool-Aid Acid Test.* New York: Farrar, Straus & Giroux, 1968, pp. 43–44.

One Flew Over the Cuckoo's Nest: Literary Themes

READINGS ON
ONE FLEW OVER THE
CUCKOO'S NEST

Defending a Controversial Book

Janet R. Sutherland

One Flew Over the Cuckoo's Nest was a controversial
source of debate between people who loved the book
and people who found it immoral and even dangerous. When the school board in Bellevue, Washington, threatened to ban *Cuckoo's Nest*, high school
English teacher Janet R. Sutherland defended it
against charges of obscenity. Calling it a valuable
work of literature, she discusses the ways in which
the book meets the standards for appropriate classroom material, according to the specific guidelines
for text selection published by the school district.

The school board, Sutherland argues, based its judgment on the book's profane language and bizarre
scenes taken out of context, rather than on the work as
a whole. The overall themes of sanity, societal "norms,"
and humanity have great merit and transcend the
book's individual elements and unconventional style.
Sutherland claims that censoring *Cuckoo's Nest*
amounts to "playing the role of Big Nurse of education."

In the judgment of one recent patron of the Bellevue Public
Schools, Ken Kesey's *One Flew Over the Cuckoo's Nest* is not
a decent book for students to read or teachers to teach.
While literary critics might be able to dismiss such pro-
nouncements as simply untutored, public school people
have to deal with them frequently and take them seriously,
in the interest of preserving their right of access to literature
and the student's right to read. It is in this context that I offer a defense of Kesey's novel against the charge that it is an
improper and even evil book, fit only "to be burned."

Ken Kesey's *One Flew Over the Cuckoo's Nest* is not obscene, racist, or immoral, although it does contain language

Reprinted, with permission, from Janet R. Sutherland, "A Defense of Ken Kesey's *One
Flew Over the Cuckoo's Nest,*" *English Journal*, vol. 61, no. 1 (1972), pp. 28–31. Copyright 1972 by the National Council of Teachers of English.

and scenes which by common taste would be so considered. Like all great literature, the book attempts to give an accurate picture of some part of the human condition, which is less than perfect. Kesey's book is set in a mental hospital; the language, attitudes, and habits of the inmates are typical of disturbed men whose already distorted world is being further systematically dehumanized by the ward nurse. The story is told in the first person through the eyes of an Indian whose health is gradually restored to him and to others through interaction with the robust new inmate McMurphy, a picaresque figure who is transformed into a tragic hero as he struggles to help the inmates regain control of their lives. To charge that the book is obscene, racist, or immoral because it gives a realistic picture of the world of the insane is to demonstrate a lack of the minimum competency in understanding literature we expect of high school students. The charge also ignores the extent to which this novel does conform to the standards outlined in the guidelines for selection of instructional materials in the Bellevue schools.

MISSING THE POINT

Our students are taught that to understand the general meaning of a book, the reader has to take all the details into consideration. The theme emerges from a complex combination of scenes, characters, and action, often in conflict and often contradictory. To judge a book simply on a few passages which contain unconventional language or fantasies is missing the point. In the case of the Indian narrator, we are seeing and hearing at times the hallucinations typical of schizophrenia. Chief Bromden has been systematically ignored and abused all his life to the point of madness. It is no wonder that his consciousness is filled with horrors, obscene and otherwise. What Kesey is telling us, beyond giving us a realistic idea of the actual language of the asylum, is that what is being done to these people is an obscenity. When McMurphy comes upon the scene, it is as if his outrageous speech and action are the only possible answer to the vicious way in which the men's privacy and smallest efforts of will are being pried into and exploited and diminished. His profanity is a verbal manifestation of the indecencies they suffer, the only appropriate response to it, a foil which helps us to see its actual nature, and a means by which the scene is transformed into a world in which some tenderness and love are possible. Big

Nurse speaks properly but does unspeakable things. McMurphy's speech is outrageous; he fights the profane with the super profane and moves beyond profanity to help the men create a new respect for themselves. He restores Harding's ability to face reality, gives Billy a sense of his manhood, and convinces Chief Bromden that he is indeed his actual six foot six, not a withered deaf mute.

If the reader is really sensitive to the specific language of the book, he will see how Kesey uses its subtle changes to signal changes in the Chief's state of mind. The fogged-in scenes are characterized by confusion and some description of the grossness of the asylum's inmates and black help. As Chief Bromden recovers his powers of perception, including his sad past and the scenes of white racism and war which have produced his state of alienation, the sentence structure and word choice change markedly. So also the emphasis on McMurphy's outward grossness shifts in the Chief's eyes to an apprehension of what he is suffering inwardly, to his deeds of kindness to the men, his complicated and puzzling deals, and his final decision to protect another man though he knows it means his doom. The Chief sees beyond McMurphy's outward geniality to the marks of anguish on his secret face.

THE WHOLE VERSUS ITS PARTS

To understand the book, then, is to experience through this unique point of view the emergence of at least three themes which the book has in common with other major works of literature. First, there is the idea that we must look beyond appearances to judge reality. Just as the reader has to look beyond the typically racist language of the inmates to find in the book as a whole a document of witness against the dehumanizing, sick effects of racism in our society, so Bromden has to look beyond the perception of the world which limits his concept of self. When the perception changes, he begins to see the reality of his growth. Chief Bromden is sick from racism and is made whole again when he learns to laugh in spite of it and to realize his identity as an American Indian. Second, there is the idea that fools and madmen have wisdom. Writers from Shakespeare to Kesey have suggested that the world is sometimes so out of joint that it can only be seen from some perspective so different that it cuts through illusion to truth. Lear and Hamlet both experience a kind of madness for this reason, madness in which it might be added, they too abandoned propriety of speech. (Polite language has hardly ever been associated with madness in literature.) And through this madness, in Kesey's book, the third theme emerges: the idea that the bumbling fool may be transformed into a worker of good deeds. McMurphy assumes almost the stature of the typical quest hero at his death. The circumstances of his life have required him to rise above the "lowness" of his original station to become a deliverer, to give up his life for his friend. The idea is that each human soul is worthy, and it is the genius of heroism to work transforming deeds which discover the worthiness both in themselves and in other humble men.

The book, then, works through the eyes and action of madmen to go from a vision of the world where all things are profane to a vision of the world where all human things are potentially sacred. Certainly teaching the book compels a discussion of obscenity, for it is impossible to understand it fully without realizing that what people do to each other in cruelty is the true obscenity, not shadow words. The book does not teach profanity; it teaches that the world of the insane is full of profanity. It does not teach racism; it clearly connects racism with cruelty and insanity. It does not teach immorality; it suggests that the fantasies of an unbalanced person are sensitive to a disruption of ordinary morality.

Frankly, the charges that the book teaches immorality puzzles me a little. Certainly Big Nurse's cruel manipulation of the men is immoral, but the young are hardly likely to identify with her and want to emulate her. Are Chief Bromden's fantasies immoral? Or are we to assume that because McMurphy is by common standards immoral that students are going out to copy him wholesale? Probably not any more than they would be inclined to copy Hamlet the murderer, Macbeth the assassin, or Oedipus the mother-lover, attractive though these tragic figures are. McMurphy, after, winds up with a prefrontal lobotomy, experiencing a psychic death as final as the physical death his friend Bromden later provides.

MEETING THE GUIDELINES

The policies of the Bellevue Public Schools provide a set of guidelines for text selection. I have tried to show how the use of this book would "enrich and support the curriculum" in English and "help the pupil improve his power of discrimination and his quality of choices" by showing that it is a piece of literature rich in design and details, and that its thematic material stands well within the tradition of great literature. As such, it clearly relates to our expectation that the student achieve minimum competency in dealing with the structure and texture of a book.

Second, within the context of that program for increasing competency in understanding literature, I have also shown how the book can be considered appropriate. More essentially, because here is where the charges against the book seem to lie, I have established a distinction through my reading of the book between the common taste which might object to the use of a four-letter word in the book, and what I consider "good taste," which will place that word in context and see its relationship to the book as a whole. I think I have established a clear sense of the difference between this book and a dirty joke. It does not comment on human experience to leave the reader with a guilty snicker of complicity in the disregard of human frailty for the sake of a cheap sensation. It deals with human weakness, eccentricity, and suffering to increase the reader's respect for the transforming power of love, which teaches us to overcome weakness, to tolerate eccentricity, and to endure suffering.

I think the book admirably fulfills the requirements of the fourth principle of the guidelines, that it "contribute to the pupil's growing understandings and appreciations of his culture and other cultures so that he can live compassionately and reasonably with his fellow men." Most students know very little about either the world of the mentally ill or the alienated condition of the American Indian. The detail of the book richly provides this information. The weaving of these details into this particular story moves the reader to deep sympathy with the Indian and much compassion for the inmates of his asylum. I think it is a profoundly humanizing book.

Fourth, and last, but not least, I would like to consider the student's freedom to read, "an inherent right and a necessity in a democratic society." I think our schools and our curriculum have to be defined vigorously against the naive reader who reacts out of a Victorian sense of propriety and out of vague fears of the magic power of the written word to want to condemn everything in literature which seems to him unconventional or strange. Attitudes such as these toward literature are a real danger to the student, in that if we yield to them we simultaneously seek to reduce the student's right to entertain ideas and teach the validity of these attitudes in the degree to which we acknowledge they have any power. We teach the student to fear ideas, or we teach the student that we fear ideas, any time we kill a book, which is after all, as Milton told us, "The lifeblood of a master spirit."

Censorship as the "Big Nurse of Education"

Kesey is a valid part of the world of American literature. His books, if not available in the library at our high school, would easily be found in any bookstore or book rack. The attempt to "protect" the students from his view of the world is in the first place futile: they like *One Flew Over the Cuckoo's Nest* and will read it anyway. Second, such an attempt would be stupid. Why neglect the opportunity to provide a framework of reason in which such an admittedly difficult book can be read, discussed, and understood—unless we want to garner the doubtful honors attributable to playing the role of Big Nurse of education, and further alienate the young people we are attempting to communicate with?

I conclude with the description of one remarkable scene in Kesey's book: Patients are allowed to vote in weekly group meetings about policies which concern their welfare and entertainment. McMurphy has requested that though the regular TV watching time is in the evening, patients be allowed access to the TV during the daytime while the World Series is being played. Big Nurse does not like this assertion of individual will which will upset the daily routine, so she opposes McMurphy and then overrules the patients' affirmative vote on a technicality. In spite of her ruling McMurphy puts down his tasks and pulls his chair in front of the TV as the game broadcast begins. It is a battle of wills, and the patients watch to see who will win. Big Nurse pulls the great lever and cuts off the power. But McMurphy remains solidly there, in front of the TV, watching the empty screen. One by one the others join him, and soon they're all sitting there, "watching the gray screen just like we could see the baseball game clear as day," and Big Nurse is "ranting and screaming" behind them.

"If somebody'd of come in and took a look, men watching a blank TV, a fifty-year-old woman hollering and squealing at the back of their heads about discipline and order and recriminations, they'd of thought the whole bunch was crazy as loons."

It is unfortunate that the patron who has lodged the objection to this book was so distracted by its alleged obscenity, racism, and immorality that he couldn't appreciate this scene. It has something to say about the need for authority to establish itself through reasonable, not arbitrary action. It also illustrates the utter futility of ever trying to get between a human being and anything he holds as dear as baseball.

Out of the '50s, into the '60s

Robert Rosenwein

The attitudes and values portrayed in *Cuckoo's Nest* have their roots in the "beat" generation. The beats were intellectuals, writers, and artists who were alienated from and did not conform to the conventions of their day. Their vision of 1950s America as a repressive, conformist society that persecuted the individual was taken up by Kesey in portraying society as a mental hospital that overpowers and controls its citizen-inmates.

The beats' response to what they considered an oppressive government and society was to withdraw from it—to drop out of and ignore it. *Cuckoo's Nest*, however, replaces this beat strategy of withdrawal with a bold, energetic activism. Rather than escape societal norms, McMurphy sets out to *change* them. Robert Rosenwein, professor of social relations at Lehigh University in Pennsylvania and editor of the journal *Contemporary Social Relations*, shows how Kesey set the tone for the rebellious '60s.

> I saw the best minds of my generation
> > destroyed by madness; starving, hysterical,
> > > naked;
> Running through the negro streets at dawn,
> > Looking for an angry fix.
> > > From "Howl," by Allen Ginsberg

The view of politics and social action which Kesey presents in *One Flew Over the Cuckoo's Nest* grew out of the attitudes of the "Beat" generation of the late 1950s. Kesey's novel is a response to the Beats' strategies for coping with a repressive society. By proposing an alternative strategy, Kesey not only aligned himself with the emerging "youth subculture" of the

Excerpted from Robert Rosenwein, "Of Beats and Beasts: Power and the Individual in the Cuckoo's Nest," *Lex et Scientia*, vol. 13, nos. 1–2 (1977), pp. 51–55. Reprinted by permission of the author.

early 1960s but also was prophetic of the strategies which were to emerge again in the early 1970s.

WHO WERE THE "BEATS"?

To speak of an historical period as if it were all of one piece and can be easily characterized is, of course, to do it an injustice. Nonetheless, for those Beat writers and poets who migrated to the San Francisco area in the middle and late 1950s, these "Eisenhower years" were both oppressive and repressive. The fear and paranoia generated by Joseph McCarthy's activities had only just begun to lessen. The "Beat intellectuals," a term which included both college professors and artists generally, were suspected by the more content members of society to harbor "subversive" thoughts. Among people in this San Francisco group, the times appeared inhospitable if not downright hostile to artistic creativity. The alienation, helplessness, and despair which this group felt manifested itself in a number of ways. If one were sensitive and caring, one went mad, committed suicide, lost oneself in drug addiction, or in some other way became, in effect, lobotomized. Essentially, the Beats felt that to fit in, to don the grey flannel suit and commute every morning to the city from the Pleasant Valley suburb, required a massive repression of all that was unique or idiosyncratic about one's personality; the only alternative which they saw to such submission was withdrawal.

Kesey must have been fully aware of these perceptions when he was writing *One Flew Over the Cuckoo's Nest.* If we can believe Tom Wolfe's account of the period from 1958 to 1963 in *The Electric Kool-Aid Acid Test,* the artists' colony at Stanford in which Kesey lived drew much of its intellectual sustenance from North Beach, the haven of the Beat generation. Hence it is not surprising to find Kesey's description of the social world in general and the social world of the ward in particular couched in these Beat terms.

AN UNEQUAL BALANCE OF POWER

When we first meet the men on Kesey's ward, we are impressed by the extent to which they have come to see themselves as victims. . . . The victim feels himself to be helpless, weak, and above all vulnerable. . . . He has no defenses against *them,* because *they* hold all the cards, all the weapons, all the resources. He, then, perceives himself as constantly open to annihilation, to death. He also lives in a state of fear and anxiety. Most importantly, he tends to perceive his victimizers as "all powerful," as "wolves," as beasts. . . .

Against this backdrop of enormous inequality in the distribution of power and control, the novel presents us with an activist strategy in bold contrast with Beat solutions of withdrawal. It is a strategy suggesting that the balance of power and control can be righted by the assertion of potency and strength against the domination of the Combine as personified by Big Nurse. The strategy is based on charismatic leadership by an individual whose energies infuse or galvanize the behavior of others. At this superficial level, one can understand why Randle Patrick McMurphy would have been attractive to readers engaged in direct social action during the 1960s. For such readers Kesey's novel might appear to be merely a call to resist tyranny and oppression, a tract designed to make us identify with the poor and oppressed and to rise up against the wicked and inhuman social order. A careful reading of the novel, however, shows that in Kesey's portrait of McMurphy is suggested a host of complexities about the style of social change.

These complexities become clearer if one explores the state of victimization in which we find the patients at the beginning of the novel, a state so intense that even the voluntarily committed cannot release themselves from it. Like a prison, a concentration camp, a boarding school, a monastery, or an army, Kesey's hospital is a total institution. It is a place in which patients are almost totally dependent for work, recreation, and survival upon the institution. . . .

Total institutions affect the self-concept of their members. A "mortification" of the self occurs, the humiliating or degrading of the self by the institution. . . .

While the other patients are "mortified," McMurphy is not. While they are intensely vulnerable, McMurphy is not. While they accept the self-image the institution forces on them, McMurphy does not. As Harding points out to McMurphy, the other patients have brought into the institution feelings of guilt, of having done bad things, of having let others down, of not having met certain standards. In short, in Bromden's terms, they have internalized the Combine. McMurphy's behavior, on the other hand, is both narcissistic and unique. He is free of guilt; he has no pressure points, no "controls" on which victimizers can play. Moreover, he goes his own way, unafraid and seemingly unconcerned about the consequences of acting in disapproved ways. McMurphy's behavior is attractive to patients beset by guilt and cowed into passive conformity. The "revolutionary" therefore stimulates the men to act out the fantasies which he embodies, that is, to be guilt-free, completely independent, and unique.

ANARCHY AND SACRIFICE

McMurphy, then, embodies for the men a counter-politics which we might describe as a democratic anarchy. Where the politics of the Combine-asylum center on total control and utter helplessness on the part of the "citizens," McMurphy's politics suggest a singular, unique, and perhaps painful individualism and commitment to the self. Where the politics of the Combine-asylum are built on internalized guilt, McMurphy's politics suggest unconflicted impulse gratification. . . .

It is a curious irony that, while at the end McMurphy has come to be deeply involved and concerned with the fate of these men, the effects of his original posture of narcissism and singularity come back to haunt him. As Chief Bromden correctly perceives, McMurphy's assault on Big Nurse, which signs his death warrant, is an expression of the enormous pressure of the men's need, and willingness, to sacrifice him. It is not unique that the most loved member of the group is set up for destruction: "We couldn't stop him because we were the ones making him do it. It wasn't the nurse that was forcing him, it was our need."

MOVING BEYOND THE BEAT GENERATION

If Kesey, then, is offering an alternative response to the Beats' withdrawal, an activist response to the cruelty and authoritarianism of the "establishment," he is at the same time suggesting the limitations of that style. McMurphy's activist style can work only if the weak and neglected rely on an heroic leader, but in becoming their leader he becomes vulnerable to the group's feelings of envy, resentment, and fear of being manipulated. McMurphy's style demands that the entire community become like him: guilt-free, independent, resistant to established authority. Yet such characteristics are, in fact, fantasy characteristics. Human beings will continue to have some socialized guilt and will continue to need to be interdependent with others. What, then, is the alternative to the cold, merciless, totalitarianism of the Combine?

To some extent, the decade of the 1960s which followed the publication of *One Flew Over the Cuckoo's Nest* can be seen as a time in which many young people sought solutions to this dilemma. One powerful stream of thought was articulated by Paul Potter and Tom Hayden in the "Port Huron" statement of 1962, which called for a "New Politics" of participatory democracy characterized by a much greater sharing of power and more equitable distribution of resources throughout the community. This "politics of fairness" tended to characterize the civil rights workers and, after 1965, the anti-war workers as well. The focus was on external change, on the reconstruction of the social structure to ensure democratic participation. Overtly, the focus was anti-elitist, and drew inspiration from the ideals of early American and British socialists.

Reaching its high point in late 1967 and early 1968, another response to the dilemma was articulated. While this response was complex and took some varied forms, at its heart was the desire to create a community in which all members were united and made equal by bonds of love. Such a community-building effort demanded not necessarily external change, but rather an internal restructuring which would allow a greater appreciation and tolerance for one's fellow men. The most visible manifestation of this "politics of love" was the "flower-child" or Hippie movement, although the upsurge of interest in communal and collective living also resulted from this feeling.

Both the "politics of fairness" and the "politics of love" were responses to the McMurphy-Combine dilemma and attempted to deal with what were perceived and presented so brilliantly by Kesey as the dangers of central leadership. People opting for either of these responses, however, were often seen to be antagonistic. Actually, they shared a common fear of any single individual, or group of individuals, coming to dominate, psychologically or structurally, others in the community or society. The political events of 1968–70—the assassinations of Robert Kennedy and Martin Luther King, the election of Richard Nixon, the invasion of Cambodia, the killings at Kent State—brought this period to a close.

The pervasive feeling of despair and helplessness which characterized the early 1970s returned Americans to an emphasis on individual change as opposed to social change. . . . The despairing perceptions of the Beat generation, with its fears of a society overly centralized, overly intrusive, overly controlling, were now more widely shared by Americans, and once again Kesey's novel was in vogue. The paranoid vision of the individual's relation to the state depicted in *One Flew Over the Cuckoo's Nest* became once again the accepted vision of life in society, and the dilemma posed by McMurphy's death was once again with Americans: how to find the balance between individual integrity and interdependence.

Comedy in
Cuckoo's Nest

Ronald Wallace

One Flew Over the Cuckoo's Nest is structured like a romance, with the heart (represented by freedom and emotion) winning out over the head (represented by the unfeeling, mechanical world). However, writes Ronald Wallace, poet, literary critic, and author of *The Last Laugh*, Kesey's use of comic devices overshadows this romantic structure, making it more comedy than romance.

Kesey uses comic reversals as a main device—reversals of the human and mechanical, of male and female, of black and white people, of the sane and the insane. In *Cuckoo's Nest*, humans are made mechanical while the truly mechanical elements are personified; men are cowed by and made effeminate by masculine women; blacks, who historically were slaves, rule over the whites; and the patients at the insane asylum seem more rational than the "sane" staff.

Another element linking *Cuckoo's Nest* to comedy is the relationship of the novel to myth and ritual, "reflecting the primitive origins of comedy itself," writes Wallace. The classic conflict between the impulsive, emotional, chaotic Dionysus and the cool, rational, orderly Apollo are well represented in the book.

Finally, Chief Bromden's narration, that of a paranoid schizophrenic, renders the other characters and events comic. His straightforward account focuses on extremes (Mac versus Nurse, reckless fun versus total control), out of which he synthesizes a more moderate view. The Chief thus has the last laugh.

Although Ken Kesey's *One Flew Over the Cuckoo's Nest* has been a highly successful first novel, a popular school textbook, an off-Broadway play, and a celebrated film, it has met with some rather strong criticism.

Reprinted from *The Last Laugh: Form and Affirmation in the Contemporary American Comic Novel*, by Ronald Wallace, by permission of the University of Missouri Press. Copyright © 1979 by the Curators of the University of Missouri.

Critics have not only questioned the book's treatment of women and blacks; they have also been dissatisfied with the hero, McMurphy, and with the "solution" he seems to offer to the horrors of modern life. . . .

Such criticisms of the novel, however, are based on two faulty assumptions: first, that the novel is a romance, and second, that McMurphy is its hero, fully embodying its values. It is important to recognize that the book is not a romance; it is a comedy. Also, McMurphy does not ultimately embody the book's comic values; Chief Bromden does.

CUCKOO'S NEST STRUCTURED LIKE A ROMANCE

It is perhaps not surprising that most critics read the novel as a romance. It is, after all, structured on the typical romantic antitheses: the self versus society, the human versus the mechanical, emotion versus reason, primitive versus civilized, freedom versus control, heart versus mind. McMurphy, a fascinating character, is seemingly the embodiment of Good in opposition to the Big Nurse's Evil. The plot focuses on the conflict between the Nurse's fixed pattern, unbreakable routine, and submission of the individual will to mechanical, humorless control, and McMurphy's freedom, self-reliance, and Dionysian revelry. In the course of the novel, Good finally subdues Evil, and although McMurphy loses his life, most of the inmates in the asylum go free, their health and vitality restored.

The novel, then, is structured on the kind of oppositions present in romance, and the final triumph of McMurphy over the Big Nurse seems that of nature over civilization, man over machine, emotion over reason. But the book's structural devices are finally more typical of comedy than of romance. The struggle between McMurphy and the Big Nurse is consistently portrayed in comic terms, and the final wisdom of the book is that of high comedy.

KESEY'S USE OF COMIC DEVICES

The most obvious comic devices in the novel are the reversal of expectation and the inversion of values, and the most obvious reversal is that of the human and the mechanical. According to [modern French philosopher] Henri Bergson, comedy results when the mechanical is encrusted on the living; this happens throughout Kesey's novel. From the outset, people become things, and things take on a malevolent life of their own. The Big Nurse is described as made of plastic and enamel, her fingernails glowing like soldering irons. The black orderlies, her hand-picked extensions, are constantly seen in mechanical terms. According to Chief Bromden, the book's narrator, "they got special sensitive equipment detects my fear and they all look up, all three at once, eyes glittering out of the black faces like the hard glitter of radio tubes out of the back of an old radio." Similarly, Doc Spivey, the ward doctor, is ruled by the inanimate. When his glasses twist askew he must tilt himself to fit them, rather than straightening them to fit him. Bromden perceives how the imposition of machines on humans renders people comic when he notes that the ward reflects "that blue-steel clarity again, that clean orderly movement of a cartoon comedy."

The reversal of people and machines is, however, but one of several comic reversals that structure the book. Male and female roles are comically reversed. If men have traditionally oppressed women, now the women oppress the men. In the asylum, the weak, ineffectual men are controlled by strong, domineering women, rendering the sexual roles themselves comic. Indeed, Kesey takes the worst male stereotype available—that of overweening power, control, force, manipulation—and imposes it on the women in the book, and the worst female stereotype—pettiness, bitchiness, lack of self-confidence, anxiousness to serve—and imposes it on the men. Thus, thirty-one-year-old Billy Bibbit remains his mother's weak, effeminate child; Harding, embarrassed by his lovely hands, is rendered impotent by his sexually demanding wife; and Chief Bromden's father "shrinks" when his wife muscles him out of his land and his heritage. The Big Nurse, of course, comically reflects them all in her paternalistic attitude and disguised aggression toward her patients. Although McMurphy admits that he couldn't "get it up" over the Nurse, Harding notes in a telling pun that the Nurse "eventually gets inside everyone."

Just as the traditional male-female roles are reversed, so are the traditional black-white roles. Whereas the blacks were traditionally the slaves of white masters, now the whites are the slaves of black masters, and Washington, named for the father and capital of our free country, is their leader.

To fault Kesey for his treatment of women and blacks is to miss the comedy of a device that has informed comic art from

Aristophanes to Erica Jong, the reversal of traditional roles. In our day the traditional roles have themselves become grotesquely comic; their reversal compounds the comedy. . . .

It becomes increasingly apparent in the course of the novel that the inmates, who are supposed to be sick, are really healthy, and the Combine, which is supposed to be healthy, is really sick. What the men learn from McMurphy is that they are "not any crazier than the average asshole on the street"; in fact, they may be less so. The doctor, on the other hand, is "a little slow in the head," while the Big Nurse, according to one of her own colleagues, is "a little sick" herself. The reversal of sanity and insanity is, then, a final comic device structuring the novel and exposing the humorous society.

Kesey's metaphor for this society is the institution, and the emblem of the institution is the Big Nurse. As representative of the humorously mechanical society, Nurse Ratched resembles the archetypal comic villain.[1] Like the typical villain of traditional comedy, the Big Nurse is a boastful impostor and self-deceived pedant who pretends to know more than she does. She is the obsessed antagonist who tries to force the plot of the novel into compliance with her own comic delusions and who, in the end, must be defeated or expelled if the comic values of life and continuity are to be celebrated. . . .

THE NOVEL AS MYTHOLOGY

But McMurphy eventually moves beyond humor to myth, reflecting the primitive origins of comedy itself. Most scholars now agree that comedy is an outgrowth of certain ancient rituals and fertility rites. *One Flew Over the Cuckoo's Nest* is virtually structured on the four elements of the fertility ritual F. M. Cornford describes in *The Origin of Attic Comedy:* the carrying out of death and the subsequent renewal of life; the fight of summer and winter, a seasonal antagonism that must end in the victory of summer over the sterility of winter; the struggle between the young king and the old; and death and resurrection, which are often imaged in the dismemberment and rebirth of a god.[2] In the novel, the Chief and the other inmates suffer a ritual death, witness the fight between the cold, white Big Nurse and the warm, redheaded Irishman, and are finally freed to new life through McMurphy's symbolic dismemberment and the Nurse's symbolic death. [Author] Wylie Sypher notes that "from the earliest time the comic ritual has been presided over by a Lord of Misrule, and the improvisations of comedy have the aspect of a Feast of Unreason, a Revel of Fools."[3] In his effort to restore humor to the men's lives, McMurphy adopts this role of Lord of Misrule, bringing the festivity and revelry of ancient ritual to the ward. . . .

As a Dionysian Lord of Misrule, McMurphy thus presides over a comic fertility ritual, restoring instinctual life to the patients. Wylie Sypher remarks that "if the authentic comic action is a sacrifice and a feast, debate and passion, it is by the same token a Saturnalia, an orgy, an assertion of the unruliness of the flesh and its vitality."[4] The final orgy in the book represents a culmination of the sexuality, drunkenness, vitality, and laughter represented by McMurphy. Mixing wine and cough syrup, and thus using the Combine's own resources as part of the revelry, the men get drunk; Billy Bibbit and Candy participate in a mock wedding ceremony, celebrating the loss of Billy's virginity; Sefelt combines an epileptic seizure with sexual intercourse, turning debility to power and causing Sandy to marvel, "I never experienced anything like it"; Chief Bromden manages to laugh in the very heart of the Combine, persuading him that "maybe the Combine wasn't all-powerful. What was to stop us from doing it again, now that we saw we could?". . .

DIONYSUS VERSUS APOLLO

But the novel is not quite so simple. The conflict is not so clearly one between pure good and pure evil. McMurphy is not merely a hero, he is a comic hero, and like other comic heroes, he reveals a decided ambivalence. As I noted at the outset, readers have criticized McMurphy (and Kesey) for his attitude toward women and blacks, for his aggressive sexuality, and for his conviction that the irrational, the chaotic, the Dionysian, must triumph over the rational, the ordered, the Apollonian. Assuming that Kesey intended McMurphy as an ideal model of healthy manhood, these readers have found Kesey's vision to be disappointing, his solution to the problems of the contemporary world impracticable and simplistic. But it is possible that Kesey himself was aware of McMurphy's shortcomings and that he intended them as a means of undercutting McMurphy, ultimately directing reader attention away from McMurphy to the more adequate embodiment of the book's comic philosophy, Chief Bromden, the author of the novel. . . .

THE SCHIZOPHRENIC NARRATOR AS COMIC HERO

Like the typical comic hero, McMurphy exposes himself as well as his humorous society. Unlike the typical comic hero, he dies for his mistakes. At the end, trying to fight the Combine with its own dehumanizing weapons, McMurphy becomes almost a tragic figure, prompting critics like Ruth H. Brady to conclude that the novel is "anything but hopeful."[5] Indeed, if McMurphy were the only hero of the novel, alone embodying its values, the novel would be a tragedy or, perhaps, a melodrama. But McMurphy is not ultimately the hero of the book—Chief Bromden is.

It is important to remember that the ostensible author of *One Flew Over the Cuckoo's Nest* is not Ken Kesey, but Chief Bromden, a schizophrenic Indian. Kesey himself regarded his inspiration to use Bromden as narrator as a major breakthrough in the writing of the novel. . . . It is Bromden, and not necessarily Kesey, who is ultimately responsible for the creation of McMurphy. McMurphy is Bromden's romantic vision of what a hero should be like, his action and motives existing only insofar as Bromden imagines them. McMurphy becomes in part a metaphor for Bromden's own development, and the central focus of the novel is on Bromden's growth toward health and a comic understanding of himself and his society. . . .

From the outset, the Chief is a comic figure, the discrepancy between his paranoid delusions and the reader's view of reality accounting for much of the humor early in the book. The Chief is firmly convinced, for example, that the mythical Combine controls everything "on hair-like wires too small for anybody's eyes but mine." The Chief literally sees microphones in the broom handles, wires in the walls, pernicious devices in the electric shavers, clocks that accelerate and decelerate at will. . . .

If the Chief's image of the ward is comic, so is his self-image. Although he is actually six-foot-eight, he thinks of himself as little. . . .

Chief Bromden is thus a comic figure, the discrepancy between his vision and the reader's and the reversal of literary conventions assuring his comedy. But if the Chief is comic, he is also a hero. Since Bromden has written the novel, it is Bromden himself who exposes his own comedy. The plot traces Bromden's growth toward the kind of comic perspective that enables him to write such a novel. When he can turn the Combine into comedy, he has defeated it. . . .

The final result of the Chief's new knowledge is the novel itself. Bromden learns to perceive his life as a comic fiction and to transform that fiction into art. Laughing at himself and his society, he writes a novel that makes the reader laugh, thus perpetuating his own comic vision. Form and content merge as Bromden writes a book in praise of laughter that itself induces laughter. . . .

It is finally the Chief, then, and not McMurphy, who embodies the novel's comic values. McMurphy dies; the Chief lives on as a distinct individual, not merely as a reincarnation of McMurphy as some critics have suggested. The Chief, for example, never adopts McMurphy's attitude toward violence and sex, nor does he reflect the machismo values of his hero. Bromden creates in McMurphy an extremity of total freedom as a balance to the nurse's extremity of total control, in an effort to locate the mean. He renders both characters comic in order to expose the flaws inherent in both approaches to human existence.

COMBINING TWO COMIC CHARACTERS
AND CREATING A HUMAN BEING

Faced with two extreme choices—the sterility, total control, and deadly order of the Combine, or the obsessive sexuality, total freedom, and chaos of McMurphy—the Chief resists both. If Bromden has learned anything from his experience, it's to be himself, to refuse to let others remake him in their image.

> I'd take a look at my own self in the mirror and wonder how it was possible that anybody could manage such an enormous thing as being what he was. There'd be my face in the mirror, dark and hard, with big, high cheekbones like the cheek underneath them had been hacked out with a hatchet, eyes all black and hard and mean-looking just like Papa's eyes or the eyes of all those tough mean-looking Indians you see on TV, and I'd think, That ain't me, that ain't my face. It wasn't even me when I was trying to be that face. I wasn't even really me then; I was just being the way I looked, the way people wanted. It don't seem like I ever have been me.

At the end, Chief Bromden has recreated himself in his own best image: strong, independent, sensitive, sympathetic, and loving, with a comic perspective on his human limitations. As an artist Bromden manages to combine the vitality, spontaneity, and freedom of McMurphy with the control and form of art. Freedom without form results in McMurphy's destruction. Form without freedom results in the horrors of the Combine. Writing a novel that combines both freedom and form, fictionalizing experience to give it meaning, maintaining the proper comic perspective on self and society, Bromden represents Kesey's hope for the future:

> The Good Guys will win. The consciousness now being forged will hang, tempered and true, in the utility closet alongside old and faithful tools like Mercy and Equality and Will Rogers.

It's what laughter can do.

NOTES

1. See Northrop Frye, *Anatomy of Criticism*, pp. 172–75, 226–28.
2. F.M. Cornford, *The Origin of Attic Comedy*, ed. Theodore Gaster (Garden City, N.Y.: Doubleday & Co., 1961), p. 9.
3. Wylie Sypher, ed., *Comedy*, p. 221.
4. Sypher, ed., *Comedy*, p. 220.
5. Ruth H. Brady, "Kesey's *One Flew Over the Cuckoo's Nest*," *Explicator* 31, no. 6 (February 1973), item 41.

Interracial Partners in the New American West

Leslie A. Fiedler

Much literature of the last few centuries reflects a
fascination with the tale of the great American West.
The West conjures up images of cowboys and Indians, lawlessness, toughness, uncharted territory, and
wilderness—and it is a metaphor for freedom and
rugged individuality. *Cuckoo's Nest* is a modern
Western fable of the outcast white man and the noble red man, who join together in rebellion against
the rigid civilizing forces of the world. These forces
are represented by "home and mother" and the "female world of civilization," writes Leslie Fiedler, author of one of the most celebrated and influential
books of criticism on American literature, *Love and
Death in the American Novel.* Nurse Ratched's harsh
attempts to make the men conform to her (and society's) ideals of "proper" behavior—and their attempts
to resist her in favor of personal liberty—provide a
backdrop for the classic good-guy, bad-guy story.

By the late twentieth century the West's vast physical ter-
rain had already been explored and little true "wilderness"
still existed, so readers and writers searched for a new and
unexplored frontier. This new frontier, says Fiedler, is the
frontier of the mind. One way to access this uncharted territory of the mind is through the use of psychedelic drugs.
Another method is to explore the world of the insane.
Hence *Cuckoo's Nest* is set, appropriately, in a mental hospital, its narrator a schizophrenic Native American and his
"partner in crime" a modern-day wrangler. As Fielder indicates, the new West is no longer geographical, but psychic.

What we demand is the archetypal account of the old, old
fable of the White outcast and the noble Red Man joined to-

gether against home and mother, against the female world of civilization. This time, however, we require a new setting, at once present and archaic—a setting which Ken Kesey discovered in the madhouse: *our* kind of madhouse, which is to say, one located in the American West, so that the Indian can make his reappearance in its midst with some probability, as well as real authenticity.

Perhaps it was necessary for Kesey to come himself out of Oregon, one of our last actual Wests (just as it was necessary for him to have been involved with one of the first experiments with the controlled use of LSD). . . .

"A Six-Foot-Six Sweeping Machine"

[The] novel opens with an obviously psychotic "I" reflecting on his guards, one of whom identifies him almost immediately, speaking in a Negro voice: "Here's the Chief. The *soo*-pah Chief, fellas. Ol' Chief Broom. Here you go, Chief Broom. . . ." Chief Bromden is his real name, this immense schizophrenic, pretending he is deaf-and-dumb to baffle "the Combine," which he believes controls the world: "Look at him: a giant janitor. There's your Vanishing American, a six-foot-six sweeping machine, scared of its own shadow. . . ." Or rather Bromden is the name he has inherited from his white mother, who subdued the full-blooded Chief who sired him and was called "The-Pine-That-Stands-Tallest-on-the-Mountain." "He fought it a long time," the half-breed son comments at one point, "till my mother made him too little to fight any more and he gave up."

Big Nurse and "Frontal-Lobe Castration"

Chief Bromden believes he is little, too, what was left in him of fight and stature subdued by a second mother, who presides over the ward in which he is confined ("She may be a mother, but she's big as a damn barn and tough as knife metal . . .") and, at one point, had given him two hundred successive shock treatments. Not only is Mother II big, however, especially in the breasts; she is even more essentially *white:* "Her face is smooth, calculated, and precision-made, like an expensive baby doll, skin like flesh-colored enamel, blend of white and cream and baby-blue eyes . . ." and her opulent body is bound tight in a starched white uniform. To understand her in her full mythological significance, we must recall that seventeenth century first White Mother of

Us All, Hannah Duston, and her struggle against the Indians who tried to master her.

Hannah has represented from the start those forces in the American community—soon identified chiefly with the female and maternal—which resist all incursions of savagery, no matter what their course. But only in the full twentieth century is the nature of Hannah's assault made quite clear, first in Freudian terms and then in psychedelic ones. "No, buddy," Kesey's white hero, Randle Patrick McMurphy, comments on the Big Nurse. "She ain't pecking at your *eyes.* That's not what she's peckin' at." And when someone, who really knows but wants to hear spoken aloud what he is too castrated to say, asks at *what,* then, R.P. McMurphy answers, "At your balls, buddy, at your everlovin' *balls.*" Yet toward the close of the book, McMurphy has to be told by the very man who questioned him earlier the meaning of his own impending lobotomy at the hands of Big Nurse ("Yes, chopping away the brain. Frontal-lobe castration. I guess if she can't cut below the belt she'll do it above the eyes"), though by this time he understands why he, as well as the Indian (only victim of the original Hannah's blade), has become the enemy of the White Woman.

In his own view, McMurphy may be a swinger, and in the eyes of his Indian buddy an ultimate Westerner, the New American Man: "He walked with long steps, too long, and he had his thumbs hooked in his pockets again. The iron in his boot heels cracked lightning out of the tile. He was the logger again, the swaggering gambler . . . the cowboy out of the TV set walking down the middle of the street to meet a dare."

But to Big Nurse—and the whole staff of the asylum whom, White or Black, male or female, she has cowed—he is only a "psychopath," not less sick for having chosen the nuthouse in which he finds himself to the work-farm to which his society had sentenced him. And she sees the purpose of the asylum as being precisely to persuade men like him to accept and function in the world of rewards and punishments which he has rejected and fled.

To do this, however, she must persuade him like the rest that he is only a "bad boy," *her* bad boy, quite like, say [Mark Twain's hero] Huckleberry Finn. But where Huck's substitute mothers demanded that he give up smoking, wear shoes, go to school, she asks (it is the last desperate version of "sivilisation") that he be sane: "All he has to do is *admit* he was wrong, to indicate, *demonstrate* rational contact and the treatment would be cancelled this time."

VOLUNTARY OR ENFORCED SANITY?

The choice is simple: either sanity abjectly accepted, or sanity imposed by tranquilizers, shock treatments, finally lobotomy itself. But McMurphy chooses instead if not madness, at least aggravated psychopathy and an alliance with his half-erased, totally schizophrenic Indian comrade—an alliance with all that his world calls unreason. . . . And this time, the alliance is not merely explicitly, but quite overtly directed against the White Woman. . . .

THE RESULTS OF CHOOSING NEITHER OF BIG NURSE'S ALTERNATIVES

For a while, the result seems utter disaster, since McMurphy, driven to attempt the rape of his tormentor, is hauled off her and duly lobotomized, left little more than a vegetable with "a face milk-white except for the heavy purple bruises around the eyes." Whiter than the White Woman who undid him, white as mother's milk: this is McMurphy at the end, except that Chief Bromden will not let it be the end, will not let "something like that sit there in the day room with his name tacked on it for twenty or thirty years so the Big Nurse could use it as an example of what can happen if you buck the system. . . ."

Therefore in the hush of the first night after the lobotomy, he creeps into the bed of his friend for what turns out to be an embrace—for only in a caricature of the act of love can he manage to kill him: "The big, hard body had a tough grip on life. . . . I finally had to lie full length on top of it and scissor the kicking legs with mine. . . . I lay there on top of the body for what seemed like days. . . . Until it was still a while and had shuddered once and was still again."

It is the first real *Liebestod* [a passionate song of love and death] in our long literature of love between white men and colored, and the first time, surely, that the Indian partner in such a pair has outlived his White brother. . . . Everyone who has lived at the heart of our dearest myth knows that it is the white boy-man who survives, as the old Indian, addressing the Great Spirit, prepares to vanish. . . .

But on the last page of *One Flew Over the Cuckoo's Nest,* Chief Bromden is on his way back to the remnants of his tribe who "have took to building their old ramshackle wood scaffolding all over the big million-dollar . . . spillway." And his very last words are: "I been away a long time.". . .

NEW MYTHICAL FRONTIERS IN *CUCKOO'S NEST*

One Flew Over the Cuckoo's Nest . . . is dreamed or hallucinated rather than merely written—which is to say, to the degree that it, like its great prototype [James Fenimore Cooper's] *Leatherstocking Tales,* is Pop Art rather than *belles lettres*—the dream once dreamed in the woods, and now redreamed on pot and acid.

Its very sentimentality, good-guys bad-guys melodrama, occasional obviousness and thinness of texture, I find—like the analogous things in Cooper—not incidental flaws, but part of the essential method of its madness. There is a phrase which reflects on Kesey's own style quite early in the book, defining it aptly, though it pretends only to represent Chief Bromden's vision of the world around him: "Like a cartoon world, where the figures are flat and outlined in black, jerking through some kind of goofy story that might be real funny if it weren't for the cartoon figures being real guys. . . ."

Everywhere in Kesey, as a matter of fact, the influence of comics and, especially, comic books is clearly perceptible, in the mythology as well as in the style; for like those of many younger writers of the moment, the images and archetypal stories which underlie his fables are not the legends of Greece and Rome, not the fairy tales of Grimm, but the adventures of Captain Marvel and Captain Marvel, Jr., those new-style Supermen who, sometime just after World War II, took over the fantasy of the young. What Western elements persist in Kesey are, as it were, first translated back into comic-strip form, then turned once more into words on the conventional book page. . . .

One Flew Over the Cuckoo's Nest survives the experiments and rejections which followed it; and looking back five years after its initial appearance, it seems clear that in it for the first time the New West was clearly defined: the West of Here and Now, rather than There and Then—the West of Madness.

The Westering impulse which Europe had begun by regarding as blasphemous (as, for instance, in Dante's description of Ulysses sailing through the Pillars of Hercules toward "the world without people"), it learned soon to think of as crazy, mocking Columbus and his dream of a passage to India, and condemning as further folly each further venture into a further West after the presence of America had been established (think, for example, of [Spanish explorer] Cabeza de Vaca walking into the vast unknown and becoming, on his impossible adventure, a god to those savages whose world he penetrated).

It is only a step from thinking of the West as madness to regarding madness as the true West, but it took the long years between the end of the fifteenth century and the middle of the twentieth to learn to take that step. There is scarcely a New Western . . . which does not in some way flirt with the notion of madness as essential to the New World; but . . . in Kesey . . . the final identification [is] made, and in Kesey at last combined with the archetype of the love that binds the lonely white man to his Indian comrade—to his *mad* Indian comrade, perhaps even to the *madness* of his Indian comrade, as Kesey amends the old tale.

EXPLORING UNCHARTED TERRITORY

We have come to accept the notion that there is still a territory unconquered and uninhabited by palefaces, the bearers of "civilization," the cadres of imperialist reason; and we have been learning that into this territory certain psychotics, a handful of "schizophrenics," have moved on ahead of the rest of us—unrecognized . . . Huck Finns, interested not in claiming the New World for any Old God, King, or Country, but in becoming New Men, members of just such a New Race as [British novelist] D.H. Lawrence foresaw. (How fascinating, then, that R.D. Laing, leading exponent among contemporary psychiatrists of the theory that some schizophrenics have "broken through" rather than "broken down," should, despite the fact that he is an Englishman, have turned to our world and its discovery in search of an analogy; he suggests that Columbus's stumbling upon America and his first garbled accounts of it provide an illuminating parallel to the ventures of certain madmen into the regions of extended or altered consciousness, and to their confused version, once they are outside of it, of the strange realm in which they have been.)

A "TRIP" OUT WEST

Obviously, not everyone is now prepared, and few of us ever will be, to make a final and total commitment to the Newest

West via psychosis; but a kind of tourism into insanity is already possible for those of us not yet ready or able to migrate permanently from the world of reason. We can take, as the New Westerns suggest, what is already popularly called—in the aptest of metaphors—a "trip," an excursion into the unknown with the aid of drugs. The West has seemed to us for a long time a place of recreation as well as of risk; and this is finally fair enough, for all the ironies implicit in turning a wilderness into a park. After all, the West remains always in some sense true to itself, as long as the Indian, no matter how subdued, penned off, or costumed for the tourist trade, survives—as long as we can confront there a creature radically different from the old self we seek to recreate in two weeks' vacation.

And while the West endures, the Western demands to be written—that form which represents a traditional and continuing dialogue between whatever old selves we transport out of whatever East, and the radically different other whom we confront in whatever West we attain. That other is the Indian still, as from the beginning, though only vestigially, nostalgically now; and also, with special novelty and poignancy, the insane.

If a myth of America is to exist in the future, it is incumbent on our writers, no matter how square and scared they may be in their deepest hearts, to conduct with the mad just such a dialogue as their predecessors learned long ago to conduct with the aboriginal dwellers in the actual Western Wilderness. It is easy to forget, but essential to remember, that the shadowy creatures living scarcely imaginable lives in the forests of Virginia once seemed as threatening to all that good Europeans believed as the acid-head or the borderline schizophrenic on the Lower East Side now seems to all that good Americans have come to believe in its place.

The Elements of Fiction in *One Flew Over the Cuckoo's Nest*

Michael Atkinson

Cuckoo's Nest has much creative energy in its dynamic presentation of ever-changing characters, in its schizophrenic Native American narrator's point of view, and in the high drama of its plot. Thus the novel clearly demonstrates the three major dimensions of the craft of fiction.

Michael Atkinson, professor of English and comparative literature at the University of Cincinnati, attributes much of the book's appeal to McMurphy, whom he calls "a real, honest-to-God, rip-snorting hero." This unusual and verbally witty figure develops, and his motivations change, in the course of the novel. Initially believing that an insane asylum would be easier penance than a work prison, he first appears as a self-centered man looking for an easy out. The events of the novel—and their accompanying horrors—change him to one who ultimately sacrifices himself to save others and maintain a moral high ground within a corrupt system. McMurphy is also transformed through his dealings with the other characters, particularly Chief Bromden.

Similarly, the Chief's character evolves through the course of events and through his relationship with McMurphy—while he begins as a weak, beaten man who does not speak, he ends as a pillar of strength who frees himself from psychological bondage. His point of view—which is also the vantage point of the novel—shifts with each new development. And underlying it all, the action of the novel likewise evolves as the characters grow and change. Atkinson thus shows how these three dimensions—character, point of view, and dramatic action—are interconnected and develop in relation to each other.

Reprinted from Michael Atkinson, "One Flew over the Fiction Course," *College Literature*, vol. 2, no. 2 (1975), pp. 120–27, by permission of *College Literature*.

Start with a full-length novel which displays clearly and dramatically all of the major components of the craft of fiction in some complexity, but in high relief—and a novel which students will devour: a high-interest work, the first twenty pages of which will compel the mass of students to finish the book in the first place and to study it in the second. Such a book is Ken Kesey's *One Flew Over the Cuckoo's Nest*, and beginning a course with it can be an entry to studying the various components of fiction in a working whole.

THE PROTAGONIST AND HIS MILIEU

The novel's central figure, Randle Patrick McMurphy, is one of the most compelling figures in recent American fiction. [He] insures our fiction against a shortage of interesting protagonists. But McMurphy is a real, honest-to-God, rip-snorting hero—a rare commodity in first- rate novels these days, and certainly a major reason for the widespread appeal of *Cuckoo's Nest*. From the first he is painted in big splashy strokes (could he be anything but a redhead?): he's a gamblin' fool who lays his money down, boys, lays his money down. Yet he is no stereotype, nor is he static. McMurphy changes during the course of the novel—from the shiftless picaro who knows when to run to the promethean whose destiny it is to remain. In the beginning, his actions and motivations are perfectly joined: his actions are the natural expressions of those motivations. But as the novel progresses, the nature of his actions remains constant while his motivations undergo a dramatic transformation.

Before his character is developed, since *milieu* [social context] defines character in *Cuckoo's Nest*, Big Nurse, the ward and its inhabitants are presented. The inmates whom McMurphy joins become, of course, the victims he finally has to save: (1) *the Acutes*—Billy, whose manhood is stunted by his mother; Martini, who hallucinates his need for companionship; Harding, who in realizing and accepting his emasculation has become a glib homosexual; Pete, who knows nothing, yet expresses all ("I'm tired"); (2) *the Chronics*—Chief Broom, who activates his reality with electronics; Colonel Matterson ("the table is *Mexico*; the pillow is a *horse*"); Ellis, who remains crucified, and urinating; and (3) *the Vegetables*—about whom nothing can be said. Though all these men may have been sick before they arrived at the ward, their sickness has been intensified and given the stamp of permanence by the antagonist of the novel, Big Nurse.[1]

THE ANTAGONIST AND OTHER WOMEN CHARACTERS

To understand Big Nurse and her function is to recognize fully the book's anti-feminism. Femininity is portrayed as a frustrating, castrating, life-denying power. McMurphy has the same desire to escape from it as does Huck Finn when he wriggles out from under the thumb of the Widow Douglas,[2] and the same horror of woman's viciousness as does the seed salesman who travels symbolically back to the womb in "A Tartarus of Maids" and discovers the savage destruction inherent in production. (Melville's tale, like *Cuckoo's Nest*, associates femininity with machinery, and loosely parallels Chief Broom's memory of the girls in the cotton mill.) Big Nurse does not attempt to usurp masculinity, but rather to destroy it by asserting feminine pre-eminence: she rests Billy Bibbit's head on her motherly breasts and gently sentences him to suicide. And when McMurphy finally rips away her starched uniform, the effect of her swelling bosom is horrific, not sensual. The birthmarked night nurse too is depicted as repressively anti-masculine: she wards off male self-assertion with a crucifix as one would deflect vampires.

The only women whom Kesey presents favorably are the whores Candy and Sandy, alike as their names, and the friendly, dirty-joke-cracking Japanese nurse. All are representatives of a femininity which is simply a receptive extension of masculine desire. Even they are presented with a sort of "good-natured" sadism (Candy's breasts are beaten red by a fishing reel).

SUSPENDING DISBELIEF

But these women are exceptions. The dominant woman is Big Nurse, the wretched Miss Ratched. Her function, as her name implies, is to be a ratchet—a wrench that turns the nut in one direction only (Kesey's governing castration symbol and psychological pun). The wrench can suffer setbacks, but the nut moves only in the direction permitted by the ratchet.

Today, even more than in the sixties when it was written, the novel's anti-feminist bias looms large. This proves to be of strong classroom use, for it brings up the issue of suspension of disbelief in a vital way. Most students enjoy the novel enormously, and yet they express sentiments ranging from

embarassed discomfort to hot outrage when asked if they
share the novel's anti-feminist assumptions, once these become explicit. *Cuckoo's Nest* provides a case in which the
process of suspending disbelief can be discussed as much
more than a theoretical proposition.

What makes us suspend our disbelief, of course, is the
sheer exuberant excitement and energy of the novel, the excitement generated by the high drama of the novel's action,
its powerful and evolving characterizations, its unusual narrative technique, and its strongly drawn symbols. When the
antagonist and her victims are well defined, when the defeat
of castrating femininity and the masculine reassertion of
freedom are clearly set as the goals of the novel, McMurphy
begins to evolve as a character; and to study the evolution of
his character is to study the structure of the novel. Part One
establishes the antagonisms and concludes with a minor
McMurphy victory: the men watch the blank TV screen on
which the World Series is *not* playing, and the cool, enamel
facade of Big Nurse cracks.

GOOD BEHAVIOR, BAD BEHAVIOR

In Part Two, McMurphy begins to develop—by retrogressing.
At the staff meeting, Big Nurse offers her definition of a man:
"McMurphy isn't extraordinary. He is simply a man and no
more, and is subject to all the fears and all the cowardice and
all the timidity that any other man is subject to."[5] She echoes
the pious moralists who can find men bearable (much less
lovable) only when they find them weak. Big Nurse continues, "Given a few more days, I have a very strong feeling he
will prove this, to us as well as the rest of the patients." And,
of course, he does. When the pool lifeguard reckons that jail
is better than the asylum—because a jail sentence is specific,
but the length of a stretch in the asylum depends on the rate
of one's "recovery"—his logic hits McMurphy (who has simply been seeking an easy life in the asylum) with full force.
Latrine-cleaner McMurphy heeds the advice of the lifeguard
(read "instinct of self-preservation"), and the next day the toi-
lets in the ward sparkle. His mode of action has changed,
though his motivation has remained constant: he wants as
quick a return as possible to the good and easy life, and thus
becomes a non-combatant.

His later decision to return to the fight, motivated by
something far deeper than his natural rebelliousness, is

based on two incidents: (1) Cheswick, counting on Mc-Murphy's support in a verbal battle with Big Nurse and not getting it, drowns himself in the pool—the same pool where, one week before, McMurphy had decided to conform; and (2) Harding one day reveals that very few of the men in the ward, except McMurphy, are committed—they stay there, suffer there, of their own free will. Later in that day Mc-Murphy "accidentally" rams his fist through the glass in the nurses' station (a glass broken and replaced three times and finally marked with a white X, forbidding, like the night nurse's cross, penetration) and the battle resumes. Randle Patrick McMurphy lives up to his initials: his constant, grinning siege amounts to a revolution per minute.

VICTORIES AND DEFEATS

Part Three is pure victory for McMurphy. The joy of the men in the basketball game and the fishing trip triumphs over the disapproval of the staff and the dock loafers. But here, too, something happens to McMurphy's ragged individualism. It is no longer his own. His boisterousness is defined by the stake that forty men have in it. His selfhood is their selfhood. The loud talk and rowdy fun are all for them. McMurphy is "dreadfully tired and strained and *frantic,* like there wasn't enough time left for something he had to do." Baptismally, McMurphy's old individualism dies, like Cheswick, in the pool; the new individualism is born in the laughter of the men at sea.

In Part Four, McMurphy the patient goes down to defeat, but McMurphy the Man triumphs. After the wild night's orgy in the dayroom, he says, "I had people buggin' me about one thing or another as far back as I can remember but that's not what—but it didn't drive me crazy." Harding replies, "No, you're right. That's not what drove you crazy. There's something else that drives people, strong people like you, my friend, down that road. . . . Us." And as McMurphy attacks Big Nurse, rips off her uniform and tries to strangle her, Chief Broom begins to understand:

> We couldn't stop him because we were the ones making him do it. It wasn't the nurse that was forcing him, it was our need that was making him push himself slowly up from sitting, his big hands driving down on the leather chair arms, pushing him up, rising and standing like one of those moving-picture zombies, obeying orders beamed at him from forty masters. It was us that had been making him go on for weeks, keeping him standing

> long after his feet and legs had given out, weeks of making him
> wink and grin and laugh and go on with his act long after his
> humor had been parched dry between two electrodes.

In punishment for this attack, McMurphy is lobotomized:
the two frontal lobes are severed from his brain in a mental
castration. Big Nurse has apparently won. But McMurphy's
will lives in the men of the ward, for they leave the institution one by one. The pattern of the death of McMurphy and
the birth of his manhood *in others* is completed when Chief
Broom kills what is left of McMurphy, then heaves the control panel through the window, and escapes.

McMurphy Reincarnated

Cuckoo's Nest doesn't end with McMurphy any more than it
begins with him. Finally, his strength lives in other men, especially Chief Broom, who exercises the ultimate strength in
killing McMurphy's remains. But in inheriting his strength,
Chief Broom apparently also inherits its burdens. This is
foreshadowed in the night scene in the Disturbed ward
when he is awakened by an inmate screaming, "I'm starting
to spin! Please look (at) me! I'm starting to spin, Indian!"
Broom reflects, "I wonder how McMurphy slept, plagued by
a hundred faces like that, or two hundred, or a thousand . . .
starved need[s]." Upon his return to the old ward, Chief is
welcomed as a hero, as the wildman who broke the arm of
the black boy. He recalls, "I grinned back at them, realizing
how McMurphy must've felt these months with these faces
screaming up at him." He too comes to understand the interdependence of strength and vulnerability.

A Psychotic, but Reliable, Point of View

But Chief Broom is more than just McMurphy's replacement
as protagonist; the fluctuating narrative mode of the novel is
based directly on his progress toward strength and manhood. An "untrustworthy" narrator perceptually, Broom is
totally reliable emotionally. When things are bad, he is conscious of the tubes in the walls, the circuits behind the
seams of the people, the descent of the entire ward into the
furnace room, the black powerhouse of the Combine, etc.
When decisions are demanded of him, he is engulfed by the
fog produced by the machines in the air vents, and when
things are going well, there are fewer machines and less fog
(not threatening on the fishing trip).[4]

Described from the outside, the narrative point of view sounds like a grotesque combination of Franz Kafka's and Isaac Asimov's. But Chief Broom's narrative achieves its effectiveness in much the same way Huck Finn's does. In *Huckleberry Finn*, to quote Richard Bridgeman, "we hear no condescending adult voice by which Huck can be judged as insufficient. His idiom is the standard."[5] In *Cuckoo's Nest* the idiom of a psychotic Indian shapes, transforms, becomes the reader's point of view, despite some careless stylistic flaws.[6]

Chief Broom's vision is credible because, first, it is based on his past. His narrative devices are based on his psychoses, and the reader-psychologist can have a field day tracing the aberrations to their sources. The cotton mill which he visited during his football days provides the source for the engine room of the Combine, and the cotton fluff there is related in appearance and effect to the fog which comes from the fog machines in the ward. Those machines, in turn, are based on the fog machines at the airports at which he served during the war. The tubes inside the people, the walls and the pills have their source in his study of electronics during his one year at college.

The second, and more important reason for the credibility of his vision is that his delusions are simply and consistently a translation of emotional realities into physical terms. A programmed, regimented, controlled society is seen as a mechanical Combine bristling with tubes; the zombies that populate it are mere shells whose seams show their falsity; the pills (or other opiates) that the Combine puts into them contain tiny wheels and cogs which alter their automatic behavior to please the Combine. EST [Electroshock Treatment] is used to recharge the more severe breakdowns. If thinking becomes difficult, the fog rolls in. When people are powerful, they swell in size; when they are about to strike, their fists become huge; when they are weak or defeated, they, like the Chief himself, shrink.

Chief's father used to be large, like McMurphy, but when he submitted to the insistence of his white wife and sold his birthright to the government she became larger, as large as Big Nurse, and he shrank (another tragedy of emasculation). And the Chief has shrunk in accepting the white man's stereotype of the Indian as his own identity. The horror of his own invisibility in the presence of the government land buyers (much like McMurphy's invisibility as a child bean-picker) closely parallels the transparency of Ellison's Invisible Man. And shades of the same despair that overwhelms the Savage in Huxley's *Brave New World* haunt the life of Kesey's Ignoble Savage.

TRANSCENDING THE HORROR

If locating Chief Broom in the tradition of the *bon sauvage* [noble savage] seems like tempting fate, it would be just as well not to talk of McMurphy as a Christ figure, or to note that he takes twelve men on the fishing trip, or that he dies that men might have life, or to mention that the EST table is shaped like a cross and the electrodes form a silver crown of thorns. Far better to play down the idea as Kesey does when he undercuts it with such ironic throw-away lines as "To hell with that fisher of *men* business," "Would anyone say that Mr. McMurphy was a saint?" and "You guys were comin' to me like some kind of savior." Far better. Yet, of course, McMurphy is the embodiment of the rough-hewn Christianity that Ezra Pound built into his "Ballad of the Goodly Fere":

Oh we drank his "Hale" in the good red wine
When we last made company,
No capon priest was the Goodly Fere
But a man o' men was he.

And if it seems best finally to acknowledge the archetypes that emerge here, then why not go on to point out that, historically, heroes sacrifice themselves to clarify the human situation, to elucidate our perception and understanding of what goes on before our very eyes and in our own minds. And that, of course, is the bond between the stages of McMurphy's sacrifice and the progression of Chief Broom's narrative technique.

The product of clarity in the religious experience is transcendence, which is usually also the case for fictions bearing a strong resemblance to ritual, as does this one. Transcendence here takes the form of laughter, a laughter that punctuates the book to affirm the horror that is there and yet affirm our ability to rise above it.

McMurphy laughs. Rocking farther and farther backward against the cabin top, spreading his laugh out across the water—laughing at the girl, at the guys, at George, at me sucking my bleeding thumb, at the captain back at the pier and the bicycle rider and the service station guys and the five thousand houses and the Big Nurse and all of it. Because he knows you have to laugh at the things just to keep yourself in balance, just to keep the world from running you plumb crazy. He knows there's a painful side; he knows my thumb smarts and his girl friend has a bruised breast and the doctor is losing his glasses, but he won't let the pain blot out the humor no more'n he'll let the humor blot out the pain.

THE INTERDEPENDENCE OF NARRATIVE ELEMENTS

When the laughter is over, the vision remains—and so does the understanding of fictional techniques. The plot, characterization and point of view of *Cuckoo's Nest* exist in sufficiently high relief that the student in an introductory fiction course can grasp them even though this be the first work he studies. Yet the complexity of the inter-relationships prevents him from thinking that there is plot *and* character *and* point of view *and* symbols, simply. Here is a chance to show, even at the beginning, how plot and point of view shape each other (in tracing Chief Broom's progressive sanity), how setting and narrative technique generate symbol (as in the creation of the Combine), how characterization can raise the questions of ideolog and suspension of disbelief (as in the novel's anti-feminism), and how myth and archetype can clarify the relation of action to point of view (as when Savior McMurphy's sacrifice ennobles Chief Brooms's Savagery). Here is a way of showing how the fabric of fiction interdepends—a seamless whole.

NOTES

1. Though the action turns on the battle between McMurphy and Big Nurse for the minds of the men in the ward, the action has larger repercussions because of the explicit links between the ward and the world—all of which constitute subversive, ironic inversions. What more perfect setting for a parable of the Absurd than a psychiatric ward? But, of course, the only "sane" men in the hospital are the inmates. And the outside world is the product of an Orwell-Huxleyan Combine. Furthermore, those who control the heart of the Combine, the asylum, also function in the outside world. Big Nurse is a weekend charity worker who delights in the gratitude and servility of those whom she benefits. Her black acolytes are men who have borne society's scorn, who bitterly hate society, and who are now the efficient means by which society is "corrected." In the nether region which mediates between the inside and the outside worlds, the doctors and nurses convene in

staff meetings which unmistakably and grotesquely embody the sweet sadism of the ward's group therapy sessions. We live in a world in which, ironically, it is better to be *Acute* or *Chronic* than *Disturbed.*

2. Leslie Fiedler notes this point in "Making it with a Little Shazam," *Book Week* (*The Washington Post*), August 2, 1964, p. 10.

3. *One Flew Over the Cuckoo's Nest* (New York: New American Library, 1963). Subsequent citations refer to this Signet edition.

4. Chief Broom is no Luddite. His admiration for George's handling of the engine-driven fishing boat demonstrates this. Machines are sinister only when they replace the soul. Also notice that the inmates, normally seen as controlled by the Combine, exercise Combine-like power of their own: Chief Broom describes McMurphy as a zombie "Obeying orders beamed at him from forty masters" (p. 267).

5. *The Colloquial Style in America* (New York: Oxford University Press, 1966), p. 9.

6. "Must of" becomes "must've" for no apparent reason. Occasional rhetorical excesses not credibly attributable to Chief Broom, such as "low, relentless, brute power" (p. 78), crop up from time to time. At one point—in describing the night nurse's daily attempts to eradicate her birthmark (p. 143)—the narrative goes beyond the limits of the Chief's point of view.

A Sexist Novel

Elizabeth McMahan

Elizabeth McMahan, a professor of English at Illinois
State University, has published several books on
composition and rhetoric, including *A Crash Course
in Composition, The Writer's Rhetoric and Handbook,*
and *The Writer's Resource: Readings for Composition.*
In this article, she asserts that beneath the positive
qualities of *One Flew Over the Cuckoo's Nest,* sexism
abounds.

In exaggerating the evils of "momism" and its emasculating effects, Kesey unfairly blames all of society's ills on
women. According to McMahan, he arbitrarily identifies
with one oppressed group, Native Americans, but not with
another, women. And while *Cuckoo's Nest* seems to excuse
the behavior of the black orderlies, portrayed as retaliating
victims, it ignores the fact that women have also been victimized and are likewise acting out their revenge.

McMahan regards Kesey's classic "battle of the sexes"
theme, with a clear winner and loser, as superficial: "*nobody* wins—certainly not women." The portrayal of women
in *Cuckoo's Nest* as "castrating bitches" can hardly be considered a victory.

In searching for positive women characters in the novel,
McMahan finds not real women but figments of Kesey's
imagination. His idea of "positive" female characters are
nurturers of men. They are good-natured prostitutes who
are so generous that they give their bodies freely and ask
nothing in return. Kesey is wrong in assuming that the oppressive Combine would change if all women behaved like
"happy hookers." Rather, says McMahan, it will change
only with female empowerment and equality with men.

Ken Kesey's *One Flew Over the Cuckoo's Nest* is a good novel—
a really teachable novel. Students get caught up in it and are
eager to talk about the characters and to explore the ramifi-

Reprinted from Elizabeth McMahan, "The Big Nurse as Ratchet: Sexism in *Cuckoo's
Nest,*" *The CEA Critic,* vol. 37, no. 4 (1975), pp. 25–27, by permission of the *CEA Critic.*

cations of the partial allegory. But despite these positive qualities, *Cuckoo's Nest* is a sexist novel. Certainly I don't want to discourage anyone from teaching it, but I do urge that colleagues should present the novel in a way that will disclose its concealed sexist bias. In order to get at the invidious aspect of *Cuckoo's Nest*, let me review the way Kesey structures his microcosm.

BIG NURSE AS COMBINE BOSS

The novel offers a compelling presentation of the way society manipulates individuals in order to keep the bureaucracy running smoothly. The mental hospital is "a little world Inside that is a made to scale prototype of the big world Outside," with both worlds being operated by the Combine, Chief Broom's appropriate name for the Establishment. A combine is a group united to pursue commercial or political interests and is also a machine that cuts off and chews up and spits out a product. Kesey has fused both meanings in his image, with the by-product being *us*—the members of society.

Boss of that "factor for the Combine" is the Big Nurse, the embodiment of the castrating female. If you're old enough to remember Philip Wylie's *Generation of Vipers*, you have met the Big Nurse before: she is Mom. Wylie described her this way:

> She is a middle-aged puffin with an eye like a hawk that has just seen a rabbit twitch far below. She is about twenty-five pounds overweight . . . with sharp heels and a hard backhand which she does not regard as a foul but a womanly defense. In a thousand of her there is not sex appeal enough to budge a hermit ten paces off a rock ledge.[1]

You remember good old Mom. Kesey calls her Miss Ratched and thus acknowledges her role as a tool of the Combine. A ratchet is a mechanism that engages the teeth of a wheel permitting motion in one direction only. Kesey's metaphor is perfect. The ward is littered with casualties of "momism": Billy Bibbit's stuttering began with his first word, M-m-m-m-mama; Ruckley's only utterance throughout the novel is "Ffffuck da wife"; Harding's neurosis stems from inferiority feelings agitated by his wife's "ample bosom"; Chief Broom's self-concept shrank in sympathy with his once-powerful father after, he says, "my mother made him too little to fight any more and he gave up." McMurphy, on the other hand, has escaped the controls of the Combine because he has "no wife wanting new linoleum."

VICTIMIZERS OR VICTIMS?

Kesey's eye is accurate in his depiction of this microcosm. The ward hums along on beams of fear and hate. The black boys are clearly serving the Combine in order to wreak vengeance on their white oppressors. The best hater of the bunch, "a dwarf the color of cold asphalt," peered from a closet at age five to watch his mother's rape, "while his papa stood by tied to the hot iron stove with plow traces, blood streaming into his shoes." Kesey makes his point melodramatically clear: the blacks are portrayed as villains because society has victimized them. They are merely retaliating.

But why is the Big Nurse so eager to emasculate the men in her charge? Why does *she* serve as a dedicated tool of the Combine? This is a question Kesey never answers; he apparently never thinks to ask it. He understands and castigates the injustice of prejudice against Indians. Remember how Chief Broom developed his habit of feigning deaf and dumbness: it was his response to people, he says, "that first started acting like I was too dumb to hear or see or say anything at all." You recall how the Indians are conned out of their homes and their way of life by the sneering, deprecating white people from town. Kesey shows himself sympathetic to oppressed minorities in our society. But what about our oppressed majority?

It never seems to occur to Kesey that possibly the Big Nurse relishes her job as "ball cutter" for precisely the same reason that the black boys take pleasure in their work. But anyone who has read Germain Greer's *The Female Eunuch* can see in the novel the fulfillment of the biblical injunction: an eye for an eye, a tooth for a tooth, a castration for a castration. Philip Wylie observed that "the mealy look of men today is the result of momism and so is the pinched and baffled fury in the eyes of womankind." True, perhaps. But Wylie thought the solution to the problem was to force woman back into her proper subservient place where she would become content again—like those happy slaves on the plantation, I suppose. And you remember Kesey's solution: Harding suggests that "man has only *one* truly effective weapon against the juggernaut of modern matriarchy." But even our virile hero McMurphy confesses that there's no way he could "get a bone up over that old buzzard." "There you are," says Harding. "She's won."

Women, you notice, keep winning these sexual battles—according to the men who manufacture them. Truth is, *nobody* wins—certainly not women. Consider how women are portrayed in Kesey's novel. We've already noted examples of the castrating bitch—Nurse Ratched, Mrs. Bibbit, Mrs. Harding, and Mrs. Bromden. Then we have the little nurse who hates the patients because her weak mind has been so warped by the Church that she thinks her birthmark a stain visited upon her because of her association with the depraved inmates. And there is the townswoman with the eyes that "spring up like the numbers in a cash register," who dupes the Indians by negotiating with *Mrs.* Bromden, rather than dealing with the Chief.

Positive Women Characters or Male Fantasies?

You may ask, are there no *good* women in Kesey's estimation? Well, yes. There is the nurse on the Disturbed Ward, an angel of mercy by virtue of ethnic origin—the little Japanese nurse. She accepts woman's time-honored role as nurturer of men and agrees with McMurphy that sexual starvation prompts Miss Ratched's perversity. "I sometimes think," she says, "all single nurses should be fired after they reach thirty-five." A sympathetic woman—to men, at least.

And there is also Candy, the whore with a heart of gold, and her friend, Sandy, who is equally charitable with her body. These women ask nothing of the men—not even money for their sexual performances. Kesey fantasizes that they come willingly to this insane asylum to service the inmates for the sheer joy of it. In his euphoric state, Chief Broom marvels:

> Drunk and running and laughing and carrying on with women square in the center of the Combine's most powerful stronghold! . . . I had to remind myself that it had *truly* happened, that we had made it happen. We had just unlocked a window and let it in like you let in the fresh air. Maybe the Combine wasn't so all-powerful

What came in through the window "like fresh air"? The two prostitutes. Kesey implies that if all women would just behave generously like Candy and Sandy, the Combine might then become vulnerable.

Changing the System

Kesey, I think, is wrong about the way to loosen the stranglehold of the emasculating female and break up the Combine.

He is simply visionary to suggest that women should emulate the attitude of the happy hookers. The truth is that women are not likely at this point to give up bossing their men around when this remains their only means of achieving a semblance of importance in society. Yet I agree with Ann Nietzke that

> contrary to popular belief, women do not want to castrate men; it's just that we are tired of being eunuchs ourselves. This does not mean that women want penises but that we want the powers, freedoms, and dignities that are automatically granted to the people who happen to have them.[2]

If the Combine could be subverted to the extent of giving up its ratchet—of allowing women genuine equality—then women could stop emasculating men and turn their energies to more self-fulfilling pursuits. Given the opportunity to run that ward in her own right, instead of having to manipulate the rabbity doctor, perhaps Miss Ratched might have run it more humanely. Forcing people into deviousness can hardly be expected to improve their character. And inequality is almost guaranteed to generate malice.

Thus we need to . . . see that Nurse Ratched is no more to blame for her malice than the black boys are for theirs. The Big Nurse happens also to be the Big Victim when viewed with an awareness of the social and economic exploitation of women. Kesey didn't have exactly this in mind, I grant, but we can still derive this insight from his novel and correct the damaging impression that the book leaves—that women, through some innate perversity, are the cause of all of society's failings.

NOTES

1. Philip Wylie, *Generation of Vipers* (New York: Pocket Books, 1942, 1955), p. 191. All references are to this edition.
2. Ann Nietzke, "Hostility on the Laugh Track," *Human Behavior* 3 (May 1974), p. 66.

CHAPTER 2

Psychological Issues

READINGS ON
ONE FLEW OVER THE
CUCKOO'S NEST

Defending the Mental Health Industry

Roger C. Loeb

One Flew Over the Cuckoo's Nest gives an exaggerated
and distorted view of mental health practices, con-
tends Roger Loeb, a psychology professor at Lehigh
University in Pennsylvania who specializes in children and the family. True, he admits, many mental
hospitals stress obedience and conformity; but he defends practices such as strict routine and "work therapy" as valuable "resocialization agents." And true,
hospitals administer medications, but based on the
medical model of treating mental disorders as physical illnesses, the drug therapies widely used today are
very successful—and certainly more humane than the
"shock treatments, straight jackets, hydrotherapy, and
surgical lobotomies, all involving some sort of physical assault," that are presented in *Cuckoo's Nest.*

Likewise, Loeb defends group therapy and a modified
form of community "democracy" used in many hospitals as
valuable because they are a reflection of the outside society; these social structures within the hospital teach patients what will be expected of them when they return to
the larger world and give them practice in interacting with
others. And while it is not impossible for an individual like
Nurse Ratched to work in the profession, the hospital staff
in *Cuckoo's Nest* does not represent the norm. Recognizing
the point of view as that of a paranoid patient, Loeb calls
Kesey's book "a mixture of accurate insights and unfortunate distortions."

Reading Ken Kesey's *One Flew Over the Cuckoo's Nest* is
likely to make us wonder whether we should have mental
hospitals. Kesey has Chief Bromden tell us that the hospital
is "for fixing up mistakes made in the neighborhoods and in

Reprinted from Roger C. Loeb, "Machines, Mops, and Medicaments: Therapy in the
Cuckoo's Nest," *Lex et Scientia*, vol. 13, nos. 1–2 (1977), pp. 38–41, by permission of the
author.

the schools and in the churches," a reasonable and important function. But then he presents a picture of a hospital with a staff seemingly motivated by sadism and with patients cowed into submission. Admittedly, this pervasively negative view of the mental hospital and its therapeutic procedures involving machines, mops, and medicaments comes from a paranoid patient; nonetheless, it is a mixture of accurate insights and unfortunate distortions. The distortions particularly merit discriminating review.

HOSPITAL COMPARED UNFAVORABLY TO A MACHINE

Our first impression of the hospital is likely to be that of a "smooth, accurate, precision-made machine." There is machinery in the walls, walls white as a refrigerator door. The aides are "black as telephones," while the chief nurse is described as being as "big as a tractor" with a bag full of wheels, gears, forceps, and pliers. When the nurse leaves at night, she puts the ward on automatic pilot. Treatment is also seen in terms of the operations of machines. Hydrotherapy, X-ray, and shock therapy equipment are all over this hospital, reflecting Kesey's perception of the world as a machine. We all start life faced with "delivery-room machinery" and subsequently we are shaped and processed for work at the mill where we return to be little more than machines of flesh operating machines of steel.

Not only is this portrayal of the mental hospital as a machine simplistic, it is also a portrayal that has become increasingly less accurate. Kesey has Nurse Ratched describe with apparent resentment the emergent "permissive" philosophy of the hospital. This permissiveness runs counter to the cold efficiency represented by machines. In this cuckoo's nest, as elsewhere, hydrotherapy has been replaced by drugs, and the use of electric shock therapy has been vastly curtailed. Many of the quick, "fix-it" machines have become historic collectors of dust and rust.

While some aspects of Kesey's protest against mechanization appear valid, Kesey exaggerates certain negative aspects of the machine. For example, consider the mechanistic coldness imputed to the hospital. Kesey's staff, particularly Nurse Ratched, is dressed in cold, stiff uniforms apparently designed to prevent any humanity from leaking out. Confronted with a prostitute, a fine anti-machine symbol, the nurses respond by "trying to freeze her bounce with a united

A Different View of the Novel's Accuracy

Howard F. Stein disagrees with Loeb about the fairness of Kesey's depiction of the mental health industry. Based on his experience, Stein finds Cuckoo's Nest *accurate for the early 1960s, when it was written. He further asserts that even though the emphasis may have shifted in more recent times away from external constraints like electroshock and lobotomy to internal ones like medication, the underlying principle of control remains the same.*

A controversy has raged over the degree to which such institutions as psychiatric hospitals are "total." That is, do they really voraciously consume and systematically extinguish the personal and private identity of their inmates and replace it with a thorough-going institutional identity? From my own intermittent ethnographic field work on inpatient psychiatric wards during the latter part of the 1960s and early 1970s, I would say that they do. So does Ken Kesey's novel *One Flew Over the Cuckoo's Nest,* which *Life* magazine characterized as an "Orwellian microcosm of all humanity, which evil personified in a tyrant known as the Big Nurse." The early 1960s were still the days of massive batteries of insulin and electroconvulsive therapy, of routine lobotomies, of the proliferation of "stabilizing," "antipsychotic" medication in the chlorpromazine series. Our means of social therapeutic control were still quite crude, and in this dawn of the community psychiatry movement, there was yet no citizens lobby organized in behalf of patient's rights. To be sure, psychotropic medication rid the mental hospital of much of its aura of repressive and oppressive physical constraints. But the restraints were not removed, only placed internally rather than imposed externally. And when the internal restraints were not sufficiently pacifying, the shock treatments and psychosurgery became the "treatment of preference" in the services of personal and social control.

Howard F. Stein, "The Cuckoo's Nest, the Banality of Evil and the Psychopath as Hero," *Journal of American Culture* 2.4 (1980): 635–45.

icy look." Kesey's view of the institutional staff as machine-like people is clear; but how accurate is this portrait outside of the fictional cuckoo's nest? Certainly some staff members in most hospitals are short on human warmth, but the mechanical monsters Kesey presents seem to be the exception rather than the rule.

Another important consideration suggested by Kesey's machines is the issue of control. A machine can maintain near-perfect control. The threat of this is illustrated by a description of "Machine Ratched." "Her voice has a tight whine like an electric saw ripping through pine" as she notifies McMurphy: "'You're committed, you realize. You are . . . under the *jurisdiction* of me. . . . Under jurisdiction and *control*,'" (first ellipsis in the original). The power of Nurse Ratched is not limited to determining the lives of her patients. She controls even time simply by adjusting the wall clock. She seems to represent various kinds of controlling forces—parents, employers, government—but these forces are all potentially legitimate and positive sources of power. Kesey denies his hospital staff the possibility of legitimate application of such control. The current movement for the civil liberties of mental patients may well owe Kesey a debt for his dramatic portrayal of the abuse of medical power.

Kesey uses machines also to symbolize society's efforts to mass-produce a standard product. The result is "five thousand kids [who] lived in those five thousand houses, owned by those guys that got off the train. The houses looked so much alike that, time and time again, the kids went home by mistake to different houses and different families." Chief Bromden holds out hope that McMurphy can resist this standardization: "he's not gonna let them twist him and manufacture him," and he will not "let the Combine mill him into fitting where they wanted him to fit." Although the pressures for conformity and compliance are inevitably great in a mental hospital, we are likely to forget that the hospital is simply society in microcosm reflecting the values affecting us all. Freedom and liberty are allowed only so long as the pertinent powers find them acceptable, be these power Big Nurse or Big Business.

"Work Therapy" a Bad Thing

Therapy in the cuckoo's nest is not solely the domain of machines. A subtler expression of Kesey's negative view of therapy is symbolized by the mop. For Kesey, the mop seems to reflect servitude. Mops are associated with the black aides and with Chief Bromden. The television uprising of the patients peaks when "we all put down our mops and brooms and scouring rags and we all go pull us chairs up." Such required work with "mops and brooms and scouring rags" is viewed by Kesey simply as another demeaning demand for compliance and as the exercise of arbitrary authority. In fact, the current name for this kind of work activity is "work therapy." Such therapy reflects the general, and quite legitimate, function of the hospital as a resocialization agent. How better can we prepare someone for re-entry into society than by having him perform the kinds of tasks which will be expected of him on the outside? In doing their work, patients can learn to follow orders, meet schedules, and be dependable. One might quibble by saying that only the most menial skills are taught in work therapy, but its goals seem far more reasonable than Kesey's vision of machine-like mop-pushers would suggest. Furthermore, there is a practical advantage in such therapy, for hospitals do need to have such work done. The legalisms surrounding peonage, work without pay, have supported Kesey's protest and the mops are now propelled by staff.

DRUGS, ILLNESS, AND THE MEDICAL MODEL

The mop is also a symbol of power when in the hands of Big Nurse. In one dramatic scene, Chief Bromden imagines that Nurse Ratched jams her wicker bag into his mouth and then "shoves it down with a mop handle." He imagines that the mop is used to shove down the third member of our therapeutic triad, the medicaments. At another point in the novel, one of the nurses is portrayed as "having a hard time keeping straight who gets poisoned with what tonight." Medication is yet another manifestation of the power of the staff over the patients and is frequently used as a threat in Kesey's novel. Nurse Ratched's perceived goal is to "tranquilize all of us completely out of existence." This goal of medicated tranquility, or tension reduction, seems to have become a national way of life, and chemical solutions to the difficulties of life are certainly not restricted to hospitals. It seems unfair of Kesey to single out mental hospitals for criticism in the use of chemical tranquilizers.

The large-scale use of pharmacopoeia in mental hospitals has evolved from the reliance of psychiatrists on the medical model. This model views emotional disturbance as the result of somatic or bodily dysfunctions. Mental disorders are viewed as "illnesses" most appropriately treated in "hospitals" by "doctors." That the "patients" often accept the model is reflected in Harding's describing the group as "'sick men.'" If such problems are indeed a result of bodily disorders—and Freud certainly believed this—then restoring biochemical balance by administering drugs seems a reasonable response.

Even if the medical model is at least partially invalid as an explanation of mental disorder, and even if the action of drugs is little understood and does not consistently lead to cure, the use of medication does seem to have moved mental institutions toward the greater humaneness Kesey appears to value. Shock treatments, straight jackets, hydrotherapy, and surgical lobotomies, all involving some sort of physical assault, have largely been replaced by chemotherapy. Drugs are also employed to calm down the hyperactive and to energize the apathetic. This makes it possible for many people to function outside of the hospital and makes psychotherapeutic procedures possible for many others. Drugs simply have a better record to date than any other form of treatment.

A PERVERTED VIEW OF PSYCHOTHERAPY

Kesey's critiques are not restricted to the use of machines, mops, and medicaments. Both individual and group psychotherapy are burlesqued in the novel. The individual therapy described appears to be psychoanalytically-oriented insight therapy or talk therapy. For example, the psychiatric residents "talk to Acutes for fifty minutes about what they did when they were little boys." The group therapy practiced seems to be a cross between a psychoanalytic therapy group and an encounter group. Voluntary group participants (and it is important to remember that the majority of the patients in Kesey's and in most mental hospitals are voluntary) are seeking a better understanding of themselves and others' reactions to them. It is these efforts, admittedly not always the most sensitive, that Kesey has McMurphy pejoratively label as a "pecking party."

The theory of the "Therapeutic Community," or running the ward as a rule-regulated democracy, is an attempt at what might called "milieu therapy"; that is, structuring the total environment to encourage openness and participation. Kesey has perverted this idea by focusing solely on the unpleasant aspects of these meetings and by seeing them merely as squealing sessions. He has chosen to ignore the potential growth derivable from a concerned sharing of perspectives and a communal striving for the best for all members of the community. The group meetings can also be seen as a form of "reality therapy." Chief Bromden reports seeing the group "work on Sefelt to get him to face up to the reality of his problem so he could adjust." Even McMurphy provides reality therapy. When confronted by Martini's visual hallucinations, McMurphy replies bluntly: "'Damn you, Martini, I told you I can't see them! Understand? Not a blessed thing!'" "'Oh,'" Martini replies, "'Well, I didn't see them either.'"

Kesey has inadvertently shown that even the hospital staff is not totally unenlightened, since "recreational therapy" (sports) is allowed. But in context, such therapy comes about as a victory of the patients, aided by spineless Dr. Spivey, rather than as a deliberate program introduced by professional staff. Kesey's misleading impression is perhaps a function of his too-simple identification of the malevolent Big Nurse with "the hospital" as an evil abstraction.

MENTAL HOSPITALS AS A REFLECTION OF OUTSIDE SOCIETY

It seems that Kesey's lack of confidence in this whole range of therapeutic approaches is based both on the inappropriateness of the methods and the corruptness of the staff members who use them. While the methods are presented simplistically and derisively, the staff is portrayed as made up of everything from bumbling fools to malevolent martinets. It is fatuous to claim that the picture Kesey's novel depicts is simply a figment of his own imagination, for many mental hospitals do stress obedience and subservience, and do violate the personal rights and privacy of the patients. Even an occasional Nurse Ratched exists to assure all concerned that "it is *entirely* for your own good." In the end, however, we believe neither her nor the novel.

A real mental hospital is a reflection of the society which created it. It is an institution embodying the socialization process of that society, and as such it is no better and no worse, no more conservative and no more progressive, and no more cruel and no more humane than the society from which it springs. Perhaps Kesey is intentionally making this point. Unfortunately, in the process he found it necessary to present a one-sided and negative view of mental hospital practices.

It is desirable to scrutinize the procedures of mental hospitals, but it is equally important to remember that the therapeutic goals of hospitals are based on social values. Such goals can never be set by the science of machines, mops, and medicaments; they can only be implemented by that science.

Kesey and Freud

Ruth Sullivan

Cuckoo's Nest defines the relations among its major
characters in terms of Freud's Oedipus complex, in
which a son acts out adult relationships with his
parents as part of growing up. In Kesey's model, Mc-
Murphy is the father, Big Nurse is the mother, and
Chief Bromden and the other inmates are the sons.
Kesey's use of such Freudian comparisons is ironic
since the novel otherwise characterizes the psycho-
analytical process as negative, dehumanizing, and
without merit.

   In this article the late Ruth Sullivan, a former
teacher at Northeastern University, discusses the
psychological underpinnings of the characters in ex-
plaining why the novel is so deeply compelling, especially to younger readers.

Sigmund Freud is something less than a culture hero in Ken
Kesey's *One Flew Over the Cuckoo's Nest*. What else but destructive can one call a psychoanalytically-informed therapy
that brands McMurphy's rebellion against the institution's
ego-murder as "schizophrenic reaction," his love of "poozle"
and pretty girls as "Latent Homosexual with Reaction Formation" or, with emphasis, "Negative Oedipal"? Kesey portrays the psychiatrists and residents as patsies of Big Nurse
Ratched; portrays her as a power-maniac running a small
machine within that big machine, Society (the "Combine").
Psychoanalytic therapy in this novel dehumanizes because it
serves not people but technology.

THE OEDIPAL MODEL IN *CUCKOO'S NEST*

Ironic then, is the fact that while the novel disparages psychoanalytic therapy, it compliments psychoanalytic theory
in that Kesey structures human relationships in *Cuckoo's
Nest* after his own understanding of Freud's delineation of

Excerpted from Ruth Sullivan, "Big Mama, Big Papa, and Little Sons in Ken Kesey's
One Flew Over the Cuckoo's Nest," *Literature and Psychology*, vol. 25, no. 1 (1975), pp.
34–44. Reprinted by permission of *Literature and Psychology*.

the oedipus complex.[1] That is, Kesey presents the typical oedipal triangle of mother, father, and sons in Nurse Ratched, Randall McMurphy, and Chief Bromden plus the other inmates of the asylum. And he dramatizes some typical oedipal conflicts: the sons witness encounters, often explicitly sexual, between the father and mother figures; and the crucial emotional issue for the sons is how to define their manliness in relation to the mother figure and with the help of and ability to identify with the father.

That Kesey intends Nurse Ratched to play Big Mama not only to Chief Bromden but also to the other characters is evident by the many references to her often-perverted maternal qualities. To Public Relations she is "just like a mother." He believes in "that tender little mother crap" as McMurphy puts it, but, the big Irishman and soon the other inmates see through "that smiling flour-faced old mother" with her "big, womanly breasts." Chief Bromden observes Big Nurse draw Billy's "cheek to her starched breast, stroking his shoulder. . . ." Meanwhile, "she continued to glare at us as she spoke. It was strange to hear that voice, soft and soothing and warm as a pillow, coming out of a face hard as porcelain.". . .

Big Nurse should be keeping those in her care warm and fed and healthy; she should be loving but is instead denying, destructive, and terrifying. Big Daddy in Randall McMurphy's Big Daddyhood is only a little less obvious than Nurse Ratched's warped maternity. "Like the logger, . . . the swaggering gambler, . . . the cowboy out of the TV set . . ." Randall McMurphy booms upon the scene, his heels striking fire out of the tiles, his huge seamed hand extended to lift the inmates out of fear and into freedom. He renews their almost-lost sense of manliness by denying Harding's description of them as "'rabbits *sans* whambam,'" by having them deepsea fish, gamble, and party-it-up with pretty little whores, by encouraging the men (himself as an example) to flirt with the nurses, by spinning virility fantasies, and by introducing Billy to women. He teaches them to laugh and to revolt against Ratched's tyranny, and he often protects them while they are growing.

---

1. Ken Kesey worked in a mental institution while writing *Cuckoo's Nest* and he knew of Freudian psychology through Vic Lovell, to whom the novel is dedicated ("To Vik [sic] Lovell, who told me dragons did not exist, then led me to their lairs") and about whom Tom Wolfe says: he was "like a young Viennese analyst, or at least a California graduate school version of one. . . . He introduced Kesey to Freudian psychology. Kesey had never run into a system of thought like this before." (Tom Wolfe, *The Electric Kool-Aid Acid Test* [New York: Bantam, 1969], p. 36.)

McMurphy plays father to all the inmates, but Chief Bromden makes explicit the Irishman's fatherly role by often comparing him to the Chief's own father. "He talks a little the way Papa used to. . . . He's as broad as Papa was tall . . . and he's hard in a different kind of way from Papa. . . ." "He's finally getting cagey, is all: The way Papa finally did. . . ." Chief Bromden learns from and is protected by McMurphy even as the small Indian boy learned to hunt from a father who tried to save the Columbia Indian's heritage for his tribe and son. "McMurphy was teaching me. I was feeling better than I'd remembered feeling since I was a kid. . . ." Chief Bromden grows big; he lifts and destroys the control panel; he frees himself from Big Nurse, the Combine, and his insanity; and he performs an act of love and mercy by killing the husk of the once-mighty McMurphy and by assuming the manhood McMurphy bestowed upon him. The big Irishman seems to pump life and blood into the Indian.

> I remember the fingers were thick and strong closing over mine, and my hand commenced to feel peculiar and went to swelling up there on my stick of an arm, like he was transmitting his own blood into it. It rang with blood and power. It blowed up near as big as his, I remember.

In fact, McMurphy encourages the Chief to surpass his model. Christ-like, the father sacrifices himself so that his sons may live free men.

Kesey sketches in the oedipal triangle, then, in dramatizing an intense emotional relationship among father, mother, and son figures and by having the father teach the sons what it means to be a man. He teaches them about self-assertion, aggression, fun, and sex—the latter sometimes in relationship to Big Nurse. After all, the inmates expect McMurphy to make Ratched into a woman by performing some sexual act with her and McMurphy eventually does that. Meanwhile, he acts sexually toward her by making teasing remarks about her big breasts. . . .

UNCONVENTIONAL ROLE MODELS

Even for McMurphy, set forth as an almost-legendary lover, women are often aggressive bitches without tenderness or generosity. When McMurphy recalls the occasion on which he lost his virginity he seems not delighted but sad. That nine-year-old "little whore" callously presented her ten-year-old lover with her dress as a memento of an act that

McMurphy had wished to sanctify. She was the "'first girl ever drug me to bed,'" he says, and "'from that day to this it seemed I might as well live up to my name—dedicated lover. . . .'" McMurphy does not embrace the role as eagerly as his boasts on other occasions seem to indicate, for in telling his tale, his expression is "woebegone" and in the dark, when he thinks no one can see him, his face "is dreadfully tired and strained and *frantic*." The event seems disillusioning partly because, boy-like, he believed that sex and commitment were complements (he proposed to the girl) but discovered that for his girl they were not; and partly, perhaps, because she rather than he was the aggressor. McMurphy jokes about this, about the underaged and oversexed girl who got him arrested for statutory rape, for instance, but the pattern in the novel seems nevertheless constant: aggressive women hurt their men. . . .

A deep disappointment that the novel expresses concerning women is not only their failure to be equal and generous partners of men or even their unwillingness to submit to men in a battle of the sexes, but their failure to play a warmly maternal role or, when actually assuming that role, their failure to play it effectively.

Though Nurse Ratched is an obvious example of this, almost all other women in the novel are, too. The birthmarked nurse, for example, cannot take adequate care of the men because she fears and hates them, holds them responsible for her "dirtiness," as she conceives of her birthmark.

> In the morning she sees how she's stained again and somehow she figures it's not really from inside her—how could it be? a good Catholic girl like her?—and she figures it's on account of working evenings among a whole wardful of people like me [Chief Bromden]. It's all our fault, and she's going to get us for it if it's the last thing she does.

Even the Japanese nurse, who has more sensitivity than any other woman in that institution, who understands why everyone hates Ratched, and who wants to help McMurphy and Chief Bromden after their fight with Washington—even she is ineffectual. Chief Bromden describes her as "about as big as the small end of nothing whittled to a fine point. . . ." She has "little bird bones in her face" and her hands are little, "full of pink birthday candles." She is maternal but not powerful enough to ensure her men's safety.

One motherly person is appreciatively portrayed in the

novel, Chief Bromden's grandmother, who, "dust in her wrinkles," sat beside the small boy at the salmon falls and counted on his fingers: "Tingle, tingle, tremble toes, she's a good fisherman, catches hens, puts 'em inna pens . . . wire blier, limber lock, three geese inna flock . . . one flew east, one flew west, one flew over the cuckoo's nest. . . ." "I like the game and I like Grandma," the Chief says, for she is a loving woman associated with all that is healthy in the Chief's background—his Indian heritage, the natural order, and the warm bond his people felt for one another. But like the Japanese nurse who cannot for long protect her men, this old woman could not save her men from moral and mental disintegration. Her son, the Chief, becomes a drunken derelict and her grandson falls insane. "Next time I saw her she was stone cold dead. . . ." She in effect abandons them when they are most needy and the nursey rime she chants is in certain ways a sinister prefiguration of what will happen to the Chief and his son. The rime is about *a woman* who catches things and puts them in pens (like Big Nurse, who pens up "Chief Broom"); about a dispersing flock of geese (like, perhaps, the dispersal of the Columbia Indian tribe and of their salmon) one of whom flies over the cuckoo's nest, over the mental institution that for the chief is both an escape from the world (a nest) and a prison. So the loving grandmother is shown abandoning her sons and indirectly predicting their defeat. Women who should be able to help and protect, or at least take care of their men are often disappointing in *Cuckoo's Nest.* . . .

MOTHER AS HEAD OF HOUSEHOLD

Chief Bromden's dramatized need for a warm mother is appropriate to his condition as schizophrenic, a man whose emotional regression is often so severe that he withdraws from reality completely (retreats into the fog), refuses to speak or acknowledge that he can hear, and cannot control body functions. The emotional pattern Kesey draws for Chief Bromden is severe withdrawal alternating with periods of intense, if often negative, fixation on a mother figure, then apparent growth to attachment to a father and finally to growth beyond an infantile need for a family. . . .

One might wonder what psychological events make the novel so especially appealing to the young (and others). Big Mama is indeed defeated and Chief Bromden as well as several inmates do escape, but the victory is pyrrhic. Cheswick,

Billy Bibbit, and most crucially, Randall McMurphy are all sacrificed to achieve that end. Furthermore, the novel promises that there will be more Big Nurses in the future:

> They talk for a while about whether she's the root of all the trouble here or not, and Harding says she's the root of most of it. Most of the other guys think so too, but McMurphy isn't so sure any more. He says he thought so at one time but now he don't know. He says he don't think getting her out of the way would really make much difference: he says there's something bigger making all this mess and goes on to try to say what he thinks it is.

Chief Bromden knows what it is:

> McMurphy doesn't know it, but he's onto what I realized a long time back, that it's not just the Big Nurse by herself, but it's the whole Combine, the nation-wide Combine that's the really big force, and the nurse is just a high ranking official for them.

In oedipal terms, the novel promises that the matriarchy cannot be defeated. To do battle with it means the castration of both the father and most of the sons; indeed, all of the sons, for the rehabilitation of Chief Bromden is fairy tale, not reality. He has been on the ward nearly twenty years; he has had over two-hundred shock treatments; and he is, by the revelations of his own speech, a paranoid schizophrenic. A man so deeply scarred is unlikely to recover so completely in a few months no matter how brilliant his model and nurturer is.

WHY READERS CAN RELATE TO *CUCKOO'S NEST*

This anxiety-filled fantasy of mechanical, destructive motherhood cannot account for the enthusiasm of Kesey's readers any more than can the genius of the style or plotting. The latter two are significant, of course, but for reasons beyond the aesthetic or intellectual pleasures they afford. The novel must somehow also create other, but satisfying fantasies and also such an effective defense against its nuclear fantasy that a reader, especially a young one, feels not only reassured but triumphant.

One of the appeals of the novel is the opportunity it affords its readers to feel unjustly persecuted and to revel in self-pity. "Poor little me. See how helpless and good I am; yet They hurt me." Because persecution of those undeserving sets the tone for *One Flew Over the Cuckoo's Nest*, a reader can scarcely escape the novel's stimulation of these unconscious feelings in himself. Everyone has in his early life experienced the apparent omnipotence and omniscience of adults who, on occasion, must frustrate the demands of their infants and must therefore seem unjust, even cruel. But such experiences usually are painful. Why should their arousal in *Cuckoo's Nest* prove delightful? Because, first, the novel is convincing about the power of the Combine and its agent, Nurse Ratched. Americans particularly have reason to feel oppressed by Big Government, Big Business, and Big Industry and to be convinced that the individual alone can do little to influence them to his benefit or to prevent their harming him. Chief Bromden is paranoic, but not everything in his vision is false: "You think the guy telling this is ranting and raving my *God:* you think this is too horrible to have really happened, this is too awful to be the truth! . . . But it's the truth even if it didn't happen." The novel offers its readers a sympathetic forum, a justification for feeling oppressed, even congratulations for being so sensitive as to have those feelings. Kesey's novel says in effect that someone understands.

A FEELING OF MORAL SUPERIORITY

A second reason for the pleasure-in-persecution feelings evoked in the reader's unconscious by *Cuckoo's Nest* is this: "Poor little me" fantasies are pleasurable if one knows that one's audience is kindly and even effective against the alleged or actual abuse. The anti-establishment, anti-tyranny tone of the novel answers these needs; so does the person of McMurphy because he functions the way a powerful father figure might against a cruel mother. The plaint of injustice is largely carried by the helpless inmates; their target is Big Nurse and the Combine; their forum and protection is McMurphy. Finally, one might speculate that being unjustly persecuted is pleasant if it arouses one's masochism and if it provides a sense of moral superiority. "You may be bigger than I am but I am superior to you in other, especially moral, ways." *Cuckoo's Nest* dramatically demonstrates the righteousness and goodness of the inmates over Big Nurse, her cohorts, and the Combine. And of course she is overthrown. Injustice may live, but in *Cuckoo's Nest* it does not thrive.

The novel also richly gratifies latent or conscious hostile impulses against authority. Obviously the novel delights in jibes and pain inflicted upon Nurse Ratched (an audience applauds whenever Big Nurse is bested in the play; it even hisses and boos when the actress who plays her takes her bow). But the book allows expression of hostile impulses toward loved authorities as well, for the inmates not only care about McMurphy, they also resent him. Big Nurse succeeds in turning most of them against him for a while when she hints that he exploits them. Billy Bibbit turns against him when caught in his sexual misdemeanor. They all use him to fight their battles, egg him on to engage Big Nurse when they, but not McMurphy, know that he can be punished in the "Brain Murdering" room. Most significantly, they kill him. They are responsible for his lobotomy: "We couldn't stop him [from attacking Big Nurse] because we were the ones making him do it. It wasn't the Nurse that was forcing him, it was our need that was making him push himself slowly up. . . ."

Chief Bromden performs the actual killing. Manifestly, the deed is euthanasia; symbolically, it is an enacted crucifixion; thematically, it is evidence that the son has grown up and surpassed his father even while loving him; and latently, the killing expresses the ancient hostility of the son to even a loving father.

AN ACCEPTABLE DEPENDENCY

To permission for indulgence in self-pity and in attacks on loved and hated authority figures, the novel adds permission to gratify dependency wishes. A theme of *One Flew Over the Cuckoo's Nest* concerns the nature of individual freedom—political, social, and psychological. It asserts that in the psychological realm, certain kinds of dependence are healthy: the dependence of a child upon good parents; of a patient upon effective nurses and doctors; and of weak adults upon nurturing strong ones. But this dependent condition is healthy only if it fosters eventual independence. Big Nurse destroys because she must control; hence she blocks the autonomy of her patients, whereas McMurphy nurtures because while he protects, he also encourages the inmates to use their own resources in order to meet the world. This theme, readily apparent to a reader's intelligence, disguises the abundant latent gratification the novel offers one's often unacknowledged pleasure in dependency upon an omnipotent figure. Throughout the novel, with a few exceptional times, McMurphy acts on behalf of the patients, acts so magnificently that a reader laughs. "'We ain't ordinary nuts; we're every bloody one of us hot off the criminal-insane

ward, on our way to San Quentin where they got better fa-
cilities to handle us.'" So McMurphy informs the gas station
attendants who would bully the inmates. Here the weak
overpower the strong the way children overpower giants in
fairy tales. The inmates overpower Big Nurse when McMurphy, a sort of kindly helper figure also common in fairy
tales, shows them how; and they overpower her in part
gayly, jokingly, in part grimly. The child-like fun of the
novel, the use of ridicule as a weapon against oppression,
and the demonstration on the part of McMurphy that he is a
bigger, better person than Big Bad Nurse all contribute to a
reader's readiness to accept the novel's tacit invitation: allow
yourself to depend upon the good, omnipotent father; he will
help you conquer the wretched stepmother.

FEAR OF LEAVING THE NEST

Cuckoo's Nest is gratifying especially to the young, then, because while on the one hand it creates an anxiety-ridden
fantasy about a destructive mother (and social order), it al-
lays it by creating a powerful, caring father. It also grants indulgence in certain unconscious needs and wishes to be dependent, to feel unjustly treated (masochistic and
moral-righteousness pleasures), and to attack and defeat
ambivalently-held authority figures (even McMurphy is
killed). . . .

Kesey's anti-technology, pro-nature theme is fittingly supported by his deliberate use of an oedipal triangle marked by
a man-woman power struggle, a triangle in which mother
acts like a machine against rather than for her children and
father tries valiantly to restore them to their own natures
and to freedom. The unconscious needs the novel stimulates
in its readers also reenforce the theme. For instance, though
men yearn to be free, they also fear it and wish to be dependent. Chief Bromden sits in the cuckoo's nest because he has
not the courage to face the world. No more do those voluntarily committed—Billy Bibbit and Harding, say, who admit
their fear of leaving the institution. . . .

The theme of *Cuckoo's Nest* is not merely the assertion
that society will get you. It also realistically affirms that if society gets you, it is because you have complied in both your
own and others' destruction. The weak are tyrants, too, subtle and dangerous because they can wake in the strong a
sympathetic identification and perhaps guilt: "Why should I

have so much when they have so little? Then, maybe I am in some way responsible for their fate." Like the inmates of the asylum, the weak can unintentionally exploit and cannibalize their benefactors, driving them to ruin.

This more subtle theme functions as defense in the novel because without it *Cuckoo's Nest* would offer a sentimental, over-simple diagnosis of an individual's ills rather than dramatizing without moralizing a complex relationship between man and his society. The novel is idealistic, but not at the expense of clearsightedness. . . .

FLYING THE COOP

Chief Bromden is the narrator; he is a paranoid schizophrenic, hence the world he describes is his world, not everyone's. Then, as the Chief comes more and more often out of the fog, his perceptions grow more accurate. For a long time he sees McMurphy as "a giant come out of the sky to save us from the Combine that was networking the land with copper wire and crystal"; later he understands the man's weaknesses; that is, his humanity. He at first believed that McMurphy might save them; he later sees that the men are using him and that they must eventually save themselves. Finally, while the novel does permit Chief Bromden to fly like a goose northward, home, it tempers the promise that Chief Bromden's freedom is hazard-free. For Kesey implicitly compares the Chief's escape scene with another in which the latter sees clearly for the first time where he is, in an asylum deep in the country. A lively, revelling dog investigates the countryside while "the moon glistened around him in the wet grass. . . ." Then the Chief listens attentively to Canada honkers flying above, "a black, weaving necklace, drawn into a V by that lead goose . . . a black cross opening and closing. . . ." Finally, he runs off

> in the direction they [the geese] had gone, toward the highway. . . . Then I could hear a car speed up out of a turn. The headlights loomed over the rise and peered ahead down the highway. I watched the dog and the car making for the same spot of pavement.

The Chief has identified with the geese, flying free after a lead goose even as the Chief and the others do when led by that "Bull Goose Loony" McMurphy, later to crucify himself ("'Do I get a crown of thorns?'") for them. He identifies with the dog, too, young and free and curious about his environment but also heading for potential death on the highway. Once more, natural things are threatened by machines. Will the Chief, too, be crushed?

> I ran across the grounds in the direction I remembered seeing the dog go, toward the highway. . . . I caught a ride with a guy, a Mexican guy, going north in a truck full of sheep.

CUCKOO'S NEST IN A PSYCHOLOGICAL NUTSHELL

Kesey does not mislead his readers. For those who choose to hear he says that while the social order is indeed a mighty, complex organism difficult to understand, more difficult to influence and change, nevertheless men are responsible for their own fates. One must be strong to survive, even stronger to prevail, but if such a man is inspirited with that most valued of American qualities, the drive for independence and freedom, he can make it.

Kesey's novel is a kind of phenomenon, though, for the skillful way in which he manages to be hard-headedly realistic . . . as well as indulgent of so many and such powerful unconscious, even infantile drives . . . and respectful of certain ethical considerations: the evil are punished, but so are those who inflict punishment: crime does not pay. . . . The fact that the theme can be doubly-perceived as that technology is responsible for man's destruction and that men are responsible for their own—this both stimulates and manages the anxiety-ridden nuclear fantasy because on the one hand a reader can fully respond to his own regressive fantasies and on the other, he is encouraged to pull out of them and cope with external reality. Kesey's use of the oedipal constellation to pattern human relationships in *Cuckoo's Nest* functions in much the same way, for by content the novel damns psychoanalytically-informed psychotherapy in such a way as to cater to fantasies or persecution and helplessness; while by artistic design the book uses psychoanalytic theory so as to reassure the reader (as all skillful handling of artistic form and style do) that nevertheless everything is safe. "I, the artist, can handle this material, dangerous though it may be. See, I make it part of the solid structure of this novel. You need not be afraid while I am in control." Mama may be dangerous, but Big Daddy is here to protect his children.

Laughter as Psychotherapy

Nicolaus Mills

The key to recovering sanity, as McMurphy offers it to the inmates, is the ability to laugh—in general, and at the wrongs and weaknesses of Big Nurse's world in particular. Laughter is such an important tool for McMurphy—for releasing tensions, for handling pain, for keeping "sane"—that he is surprised by the utter lack of it in such a place as the mental ward. Hence his crusade to use laughter as a way of encouraging the inmates to regain their mental freedom. The men slowly come to recognize that a power transfer seems to take place between them and Big Nurse when their laughter disrupts her authority.

Nicolaus Mills, author of *The Crowd in American Literature* (1986), discusses McMurphy's credo that while laughter does not prevent death and failure, it helps to keep death and failure from overwhelming us.

The marrow of Kesey's art in *One Flew Over the Cuckoo's Nest* lies in his description of a struggle for sanity. . . . Chief Bromden, Kesey's Indian narrator, . . . is the schizophrenic inmate of an insane asylum, a victim of "more than two hundred shock treatments," who docilely does the cleaning on his ward. . . .

The Chief's illness, which causes him to fake being deaf and dumb, stems from his overriding sense of trappedness. Despite his size, the Chief is sure his strength is unequal to any task he faces. He imagines himself under the influence of an organization called the Combine, which has the power to baffle his senses with a fog machine and control his movements with "hairlike wires too small for anybody [else's] eyes" to notice. Kesey undertakes in exploring the Chief's fears to reproduce the logic of his experience rather

Excerpted from Nicolaus Mills, "Ken Kesey and the Politics of Laughter," *The Centennial Review*, vol. 16, no. 1 (1972), pp. 82–90. Reprinted with permission.

than analyze it away. Like [psychiatrist] R.D. Laing in *The Politics of Experience* Kesey finds a basic validity in the response the schizophrenic makes to life, especially when the response involves "a successful attempt not to adapt to pseudo-social realities." The Chief's narration of his story, while often confusing, represents a breakthrough rather than a breakdown. As Randle McMurphy, the man who helps the Chief get control of his life, observes after one of their conversations, "I didn't say it didn't make sense Chief, I just said it was talkin crazy."

Defining "Sanity"

In clinical terms the connection Kesey draws between the Chief's adult fears and his childhood memories is an orthodox one. When the Chief thinks of his past, it is almost always with a feeling of humiliation. . . . Kesey's primary emphasis is not, however, on the racial origins of the Chief's schizophrenia but on the broader relationship between sanity and political control that his schizophrenia reveals: specifically, a situation in which, to quote R. D. Laing again:

> The "normally" alienated person, by reason of the fact that he acts more or less like everyone else, is taken to be sane. Other forms of alienation that are out of step with the prevailing state of alienation are . . . labelled by the "normal" majority as bad or mad.

Early in the novel, the Chief makes it clear how often he and his fellow inmates have been given a political definition of sanity:

> I've heard that theory of the Therapeutic Community enough times to repeat it forwards and backwards—how a guy has to learn to get along in a group before he'll be able to function in a normal society; how the group can help the guy by showing him where he's out of place; how society is what decides who's sane and who isn't, so you got to measure up.

The asylum in which the Chief has been confined since the end of World War II has no intention of freeing him or anyone else seriously opposed to the way society is run. "You men are in this hospital . . . because of your proven inability to adjust to society," Miss Ratched, the Big Nurse of the ward, tells her patients as she struggles to make them conform. . . .

Kesey is ultimately concerned with why people like the Chief are driven "insane" and why people like McMurphy are not. The key to this dilemma is supplied by Dale Harding, the most intellectual of the patients on Big Nurse's ward. As Harding notes, what distinguishes the men on the ward is neither their eccentricity nor their weakness but their inability to face their weakness: "All of us here are rabbits of varying ages and degrees, hippity-hopping through our Walt Disney World. Oh, don't misunderstand me, we're not in here *because* we are rabbits . . . we're all in here because we can't *adjust* to our rabbithood." Harding's views are confirmed both by the histories of the men and McMurphy's observation, "I been surprised how sane you guys are. As near as I can tell you're not any crazier than the average asshole on the street." The significance of Harding's and Kesey's analysis is that it makes the problem of the men's sanity a question of whether or not they can do something about their rabbithood: in this case, end their passivity and defy Big Nurse and the Combine. Such a view does not preclude the need for constructive therapy or traditional revolution, but it suggests that at present the men need to undertake more concrete, less grandiose action. It is this action, as personified by McMurphy's rebellion, that constitutes Kesey's politics of laughter: a comedy that at one level seeks to demonstrate the weaknesses (not merely the wrongs) of Big Nurse's world and at another level offers the men immersed in that world the courage to accept their freedom.

LAUGHTER AS LIBERTY

For McMurphy, laughter is above all functional. It does not simply provide a release of tensions but a way of gaining one's balance so that he can deal with pain. As the Chief discovers, "he knows you have to laugh at things that hurt you just to keep yourself in balance, just to keep the world from running you plumb crazy." It is this absence of laughter that McMurphy immediately notices when he comes on the ward:

> You know, that's the first thing that got me about this place, that there wasn't anybody laughing. I haven't heard a real laugh since I came through that door, do you know that? Man, when you lose your laugh you lose your footing. A man go around lettin' a woman whup him till he can't laugh any more, and he loses one of the biggest edges he's got on his side.

Getting the men to laugh is a difficult task, however. For it is not a question of amusing them but making them see there is a comedy in their situation that originates with the assumption their behavior is insane while that of society is sane. In his first day on the ward McMurphy shows his disdain for this distinction by asking, "Which one of you claims to be the craziest? Which one is the biggest looney?" When told that Harding is the "Bull Goose Loony," McMurphy sets up the counterclaim that he is and confesses, "I'm so crazy I admit to voting for Eisenhower." Harding can only reply, "I'm so crazy I voted for Eisenhower twice." The argument is one that neither Harding nor McMurphy can really win, but it has the effect of giving the men a new and amused perspective of the arbitrary way they have been categorized.

Without this perspective the men cannot begin to act, but the perspective is still a limited one. It does not change the fact that the men "look spooked and uneasy" when McMurphy laughs, "the way kids look in a schoolroom when one onery kid is raising too much hell with the teacher out of the room and they're all scared the teacher might pop back in and . . . make them all stay after." For the men's laughter to become truly liberating, they must also see that Big Nurse can be defied, that her control, like the label of insanity they have been given, can be punctured and in the process made comic. The defiance McMurphy organizes against Big Nurse is aimed to "Bug her till she comes apart at those neat little seams, and shows, just one time, she ain't so unbeatable as you think." The defiance takes the form of a guerrilla action with the men shamming forgetfulness and stupidity and on occasion calling Big Nurse's bluff by asking for a vote on rules. It culminates with those living under Big Nurse's rule realizing the degree to which they have policed themselves and defying her ban on watching the World Series. Even when Big Nurse turns the television off, the men remain confident enough of their sense of reality to sit with McMurphy in front of the blank screen and pretend to be enjoying the game:

> And we're all sitting there lined up in front of that blanked out TV set, watching the gray screen just like we could see the baseball game clear as day, and she's ranting and screaming behind us.
>
> If somebody'd of come in and took a look, men watching a blank TV, a fifty-year-old woman hollering and squealing at the back of their heads about discipline and order and recriminations, they'd of thought the whole bunch was crazy as loons.

The Politics of Laughter: A Transfer of Power

Big Nurse does not give up her authority after this defeat or even after McMurphy organizes a salmon fishing trip in which the men find they can survive in the outside world. But once the men have learned to laugh at the way they are looked at and treated, Big Nurse's power is over. She cannot regain it by removing McMurphy from the ward. "She tried to get her ward back into shape, but it was difficult with Mc-Murphy's presence still tromping up and down the halls and laughing out loud in the meetings and singing in the latrines. She couldn't rule with her old power any more. . . ." The question that remains is: How deeply internalized is McMurphy's laughter? How much are the men now acting on their own?

Certainly, McMurphy has every opportunity to appear to the men as a God. When he is punished by being given extra electric shock therapy, he is literally put in the position of a Christ, "strapped to a table, shaped, ironically like a cross, with a crown of electric sparks in place of thorns." But to see McMurphy as a Christ is to misread the point of his and Kesey's humor. McMurphy's laughter does not rise from a sense of superiority but from a belief in the sufficiency of his and others' humanness. He sees his punishment as a parody rather than a duplication of Christ's:

> They put the graphite salve on his temples. "What is it?" he says. "Conductant," the technican says. "Anointest my head with conductant. Do I get a crown of thorns?"

> They smear it on. He's singing to them, makes their hands shake.

> "'Get Wildroot Cream Oil, Cholly. . . .'"

The result is that McMurphy is able to convince the men that the kinds of strengths he possesses are also theirs, for at the time of his most intense suffering he reveals anything but suprahuman qualities. Harding is correct when he tells Mc-Murphy the men are no longer rabbits, and the Chief provides the most telling proof of how effective McMurphy's laughter has been.

The Chief learns to laugh before he relearns to speak and does so by directing his most important laughter at himself. The turning point comes when McMurphy, who always talks to the Chief as if he were not deaf and dumb, asks him about his habit of hiding gum he finds under his bed:

> "Chief?" McMurphy whispered. "I want you to tell me something." And he started to sing a little song, a hillbilly song, popular a long time ago: "'Oh, does the Spearmint lose its flavor on the bedpost overnight?'"

> At first I started getting real mad. I thought he was making fun of me like other people had.
>
> "'When you chew it in the morning,'" he sang in a whisper, "'will it be too hard to bite?'"
>
> But the more I thought about it the funnier it seemed to me. I tried to stop it but I could feel I was about to laugh—not at McMurphy's singing, but at my own self.

As epiphanies go, the Chief's is certainly without grandeur, but this, too, is McMurphy's point. "He won't let the pain blot out the humor no more'n he'll let the humor blot out the pain." The Chief's laughter makes sense precisely because he has come to acknowledge the ridiculous aspect of his behavior in such a way that the acknowledgment itself is a sign of his strength and his release from the past. In the end, when the Chief escapes from the asylum, he does it by breaking a heavily screened window with the same control panel McMurphy bet the men he could pick up and then failed to lift off the floor. The Chief's triumph at this point is the final demonstration of how fully he and the others have come to embody McMurphy's politics of laughter: to recognize that it was not intended to eliminate death and failure but to show that death and failure need not prevent them from acting.

Personal Identity and Spiritual Rebirth

Ellen Herrenkohl

McMurphy is the hero of an external political struggle that ends in his death; Chief Bromden is the hero of an internal psychological struggle ending in his rebirth. As McMurphy sacrifices his own identity as hustler/survivor and accepts the role of martyr, the Chief recovers his personal identity through his restored childhood memories, which signals a renewal of life.

Ellen Herrenkohl, who holds a Ph.D. from Tufts University and conducts research on family interactions, addresses ways the mental health industry views and treats its wards: depriving them of the most basic privacy, robbing them of personal ambition, treating them like children instead of adults, and behaving as if they were invisible. Yet in assigning blame for the state of things, she also implicates the patients themselves as accomplices, emphasizing that going along with the system is the same as enabling it. Free will, says Herrenkohl, plays an important role in lifting oneself out of a mental "fog." This is clearly demonstrated by Chief Bromden, who in the end takes personal responsibility and, with no help from the institution, is able to "smell the breeze" for the first time in years.

Chronic schizophrenics are "machines with flaws inside that can't be repaired, flaws born in, or flaws beat in," Chief Bromden tells us early in *One Flew Over the Cuckoo's Nest*. His definition reflects the resignation of patients and staff to a belief in individual helplessness and powerlessness. The entrance of McMurphy into the hospital scene sets the stage for the struggle between a resignation to external control and a striving for the stamp of individual control. The novel

Reprinted from Ellen Herrenkohl, "Regaining Freedom: Sanity in Insane Places," *Lex et Scientia*, vol. 13, nos. 1–2 (1977), pp. 42–44, by permission of the author.

contains two dramas within this theme: the external struggle of the individual against the insanity of a machine-like
environment in which he is caught; and the internal struggle of the individual for sanity through achieving a sense of
personal reality. McMurphy dies as the hero of the former;
Chief Bromden is reborn as the hero of the latter. It is this
second drama that I shall focus on in this paper.

SOLITUDE AS SICKNESS

The "institution" communicates and reinforces the notion of
individual powerlessness in several ways. First, there is the
stripping, literally and figuratively, of privacy and individuality. The "admission rites" to the ward include the subjec-
tion of the new inmate to the required shower: "The black
boys come sign for him . . . and leave him shivering with the
door open while they all three run grinning up and down the
halls looking for the Vaseline." The "log book" is the loud-
speaker for any personal information which leaks into the
"therapeutic atmosphere" of the ward. "Talk," says the doctor, "discuss, confess. And if you hear a friend say something
during the course of your everyday conversation, then list it
in the log book for the staff to see. . . . Bring these old sins
into the open where they can be washed by the sight of
all. . . . There should be no need for secrets among friends."

The desire to be alone is seen as "sick." The nurses sit behind their glass wall and watch every movement of the patients in their therapeutic fishbowl. Nurse Ratched capital-
izes on the phenomenon psychoanalyst Erich Fromm
depicts as a central ailment of modern society: the loss of
personal identity which makes conformity a necessity as
one substitutes the expectations of others for the deteriorat-
ing sense of one's own standards and goals. She preaches
the therapeutic necessity of togetherness: "'The doctor and I
believe that every minute spent in the company of others,
with some exceptions, is therapeutic, while every minute
spent brooding alone only increases your separation.'"

MATURITY, MOTIVATION, AND INVISIBILITY

The patients are robbed not only of privacy but also of maturity. Nurse Ratched calls her patients "boys" and addresses
each as if he were "nothing but a three-year-old." Childlike
helplessness is dictated at every turn by the staff. Routines
are enforced at all costs. Only patient Taber has dared to ask

the nature of the medication he is required to swallow and thereby has set himself up for a further lesson in enforced helplessness through lobotomy. McMurphy is "sentenced" to

QUESTIONING THE CHIEF'S REBIRTH

Not all readers find the Chief's final "escape" to be as meaningful as Herrenkohl does. Critic Ruth H. Brady takes a much dimmer view of the Chief's future.

At one point in the novel, when Chief reaches a point of sensual awareness and begins to feel, see, and smell things, he looks through a window and notices an inquisitive dog outside, running about freely as he goes about nighttime discoveries in the glistening moonlight, investigating new sounds and odors. At that moment, a flock of Canada honkers flying across the moonlit sky catches the dog's attention, and when they are past, the dog runs in their direction:

> . . . When he couldn't hear them any more either, he commenced to lope off in the direction they had gone, toward the highway, loping steady and solemn like he had an appointment. I held my breath and I could hear the flap of his big paws on the grass as he loped; then I could hear a car speed up out of a turn. The headlights loomed over the rise and peered ahead down the highway. I watched the dog and the car making for the same spot of pavement.

Certainly the reader can only believe that this free dog is headed for a rendezvous with destruction.

This dog episode is so important to the novel's meaning that, on the last page of the novel, after Chief heaves the control panel through the window and leaves the institution, the author has Chief think again of this dog:

> . . . I ran across the grounds in the direction I remembered seeing the dog go, toward the highway . . . I felt like I was flying. Free.

To assume that Chief escapes to total freedom is, I believe, a misinterpretation of the novel's theme. Imagistically, Chief, like the free dog, enjoys a momentary freedom; but the dog heads toward the highway, and therefore toward destruction, the same direction, incidentally, which the Canada honkers flew when they flew across the moon, with the "lead goose" forming a "black cross" against the moon as a dire warning. . . .

The novel's entire meaning becomes twisted if Chief's "escape" is interpreted optimistically. He has simply gone "Outside," where the Combine still rules. He has escaped from one cage into a larger one.

Brady, Ruth H. "Kesey's *One Flew Over the Cuckoo's Nest.*" *Explicator* 31.6 (1973): 41.

an undetermined number of months or years on the ward much as a child is banished to his room for misbehavior by an arbitrary authority figure.

The label of "insanity" is used to prejudice the meaning of human behavior. "Motivation" is seen to be limited to the self-centered drives of immature and unsocialized beings or the incomprehensible drives of insanity. When the naive Nurse Flinn asks Big Nurse why a man would seek to disrupt the ward, she gets this reply: "'You seem to forget, *Miss* Flinn, that this is an institution for the insane.'" Even laughter is taken to be the outbreak of an irrational, uncontrollable, and therefore undesirable symptom.

The ultimate lesson in dehumanization is the "invisible treatment." Not only are the patients treated as if they lack private history, meaningful behavior, maturity, and ability to reason, but they are even responded to as if they lacked material substance. Chief Bromden pushes his broom through the rooms and halls, unnoticed: "they see right through me like I wasn't there—the only thing they'd miss if I didn't show up would be the sponge and the water bucket floating around."

"Real Life" provides a recent analogue to Chief Bromden's fictional situation. In an experiment conducted by researcher D.L. Rosenhan, eight sane people gained secret admission to mental hospitals in five different states by posing as psychotics. The experiment raised strong questions about the meaning of the term "insanity." After an initial complaint at the admissions desk about "hearing voices," each pseudopatient ceased pretending any symptoms of psychosis during his hospitalization. Yet, not one was detected as sane by the staff and each was discharged with a diagnosis of "schizophrenia in remission." The power of the label was such that innocent behavior, even note-taking, was viewed by the staff as pathological. Interestingly, Rosenhan, who himself participated in the experiment, confesses to have experienced the same sensation of invisibility which Chief Bromden describes: "A nurse unbuttoned her uniform to adjust her brassiere in the presence of an entire ward of viewing men. One did not have the sense she was being seductive. Rather, she didn't notice us. A group of staff persons might point to a patient in the dayroom and discuss him animatedly, as if he were not there." Kesey's "fiction" assumed a reality of bizarre proportions in this factual study. We are forced by Kesey to ask the same question that Rosenhan has asked: "How many patients might be 'sane' outside the psychiatric hospital, but seem insane in it—not because craziness resides in them, as it were, but because they are responding to a bizarre setting" in which emotional avoidance, physical mistreatment, and psychological abuse depersonalize patients.[1]

Who and What Are to Blame

The institution has its methods of dehumanizing and deindividuating, but its victims are not without some share of the blame. The patients in Kesey's novel contribute to the process of dehumanization. First, they are eager to view themselves as controlled by forces beyond human control. They behave as if they have been committed and as if the duration of their "sentence" is up to the decision of the authorities. To McMurphy's amazement, it turns out that most of them are there because they have sought admission, and are too frightened to leave.

The "fog," which rolls in and descends on Chief Bromden encapsulating him and making motion difficult and vision unclear, is in actuality a barrier which he pulls down around himself to protect himself and create a cave of safety. The boredom from which he suffers is a symptom, not of disease, but of a deficiency in his own sense of control. Time comes to a dead stop and "freezes" or inches by, controlled, in Chief Bromden's view, not by his own unwillingness to involve himself in the external world, but by the movement of others. Chief Bromden eventually, however, comes to the realization that his invisibility has been in part a product of his own making, and that others begin to act as if he could not hear in part because he behaves as if he did not hear.

Blaming genetic inheritance is another form of eager resignation to external control. "'I was born dead. . . . I can't help it. I was born a miscarriage,'" cries Bancini. "'I was born a rabbit,'" states Harding, hoping to defend his role of passivity, and to blame his fear on the "'law of the natural world. . . . We mustn't be ashamed of our behavior; it's the way we little animals were meant to behave.'" McMurphy, of course, sees that blaming inheritance is mostly self-deception.

---

1. D.L Rosenhan, "On Being Sane in Insane Places," *Science*, Vol. 179, no. 4070, pp. 256–57.

The "victims" of the Combine are not only the hospital patients, but the hospital staff as well, the authority figures who run the machinery and monitor its dehumanizing process. The dehumanizing rules they enforce serve to dehumanize themselves as well by providing them with a defense against recognition of their own individuality, emotionality, and sexuality. There are many examples: the young nurse's embarrassment at McMurphy's provocative teasing; Dr. Spivey's frightened lack of manhood; Big Nurse's attempt to rise above sex and human warmth.

THE FOG LIFTS

What is the safety that the fog and boredom and prisoner mentality provide? Against what does the adherence and submission to helplessness protect its victims? Chief Bromden grasps the meaning of the fog. McMurphy, he tells us, "keeps trying to drag us out of the fog, out in the open where we'd be easy to get at." To see clearly, to be seen clearly, is to be vulnerable. To admit to oneself one's feelings and one's perceptions is to be open to disappointment, to fear, to rejection, to rage, to guilt, to tragedy.

McMurphy pulls Chief Bromden and his fellow patients out of the timeless fog in which they are submerged by assuming that men *do* have choices in life. This con artist assumes that Chief Bromden's deaf-dumb posture is a conscious pose. From the beginning "he wasn't fooled for one minute by my deaf-and-dumb act; it didn't make any difference *how* cagey the act was, he was onto me and was laughing and winking to let me know it."

The uneducated McMurphy understands the meaningfulness of "crazy" behavior. Insanity is not an explanation of anything for him, a dead-end label, an excuse. To be crazy is to be not without sense, but without guts. Chief Bromden comes to share McMurphy's point of view. Colonel Matterson, who began spouting "crazy talk" six years earlier, suddenly takes on a new dimension for Chief Bromden: "'I never paid him any mind, figured he was no more than a talking statue, a thing made out of bone and arthritis, rambling on and on with these goofy definitions of his that didn't make a lick of sense. Now, at last, I see what he's saying. . . . You're making sense, old man, a sense of your own.'"

In a supremely ironic twist, McMurphy the psychopath, the manipulator without a conscience, gives the inmates back their capacity for feeling guilt; for guilt is not possible without a sense of having chosen, of having decided, without a sense of freedom. McMurphy castigates the Acutes for cowardice, rather than excuses them because of illness. "'I ain't so sure but what they should be ashamed,'" he rages. His rage is based on the assumption that the patients are responsible men.

FEELING THE FLOOR FOR THE FIRST TIME

What do we gain with acceptance of responsibility and of vulnerability? Chief Bromden lets us in on the discovery in his climb out of the fog. One night, when "for the first time in years I was seeing people with none of that black outline they used to have," he slid out of bed. "I felt the tile with my feet and wondered how many times, how many thousand times, had I run a mop over this same tile floor and never felt it at all. . . . I smelled the breeze." Chief Bromden then suddenly finds himself in touch with childhood memories which had been previously lost in the fog. The reborn narrator sees and smells and feels and remembers, recapturing a sense of personal reality.

Chief Bromden thus reaches instinctively for the Frommian insight that man "would be free to act according to his own will, if he knew what he wanted, thought, and felt."[2] Chief Bromden prepares, by reaching back inside himself, to touch base with his yearnings and his wounds. He is ready to accomplish what Fromm calls "man's main task in life": "to give birth to himself, to become what he potentially is."[3] Bromden is the hero of the second drama of the novel precisely because he emerges with the necessary condition of sanity—a sense of personal identity.

---

2. Erich Fromm, *Escape from Freedom* (New York: Rinehart, 1941), p. 255. 3. Erich Fromm, *Man for Himself* (New York: Rineheart, 1947), p. 237.

CHAPTER 3

Characters in *Cuckoo's Nest*

READINGS ON

ONE FLEW OVER THE

CUCKOO'S NEST

McMurphy as Revolutionary Hero

Jerome Klinkowitz

Jerome Klinkowitz, professor of English at the University of Northern Iowa and author of more than thirty books on contemporary culture, calls the literary characters McMurphy and Yossarian (the protagonist of Joseph Heller's *Catch-22*) "culture heroes of the bold new decade of the American 1960s." *Cuckoo's Nest* and *Catch-22* were "underground novels," which gained a following by word of mouth independently of the mass media. At a time when more young people than ever before were entering colleges, both books were popular campus novels, taught by equally young baby boomer teaching assistants to a generation of students who would come to identify with protest and revolution.

Here, Klinkowitz discusses the complex character of McMurphy, his quest for spiritual over material "prosperity," and his humane attempts to transform the inmates' perceived weaknesses into strengths. The ways in which McMurphy seeks to "buck the system" spoke directly to those students reading *Cuckoo's Nest* in college classrooms throughout the country during the 1960s.

Randall Patrick McMurphy, the small-time gambler and brawler who seeks relief from prison work-farm drudgery by bluffing his way into a mental asylum, and Captain Yossarian, an Air Corps bombardier who thinks people (such as German gunners) are trying to kill him, are political forces within their own novels. McMurphy leads an open rebellion against the ward's authoritarian head nurse, and Yossarian debates conventional notions of authority, and even rational order, in war. Beyond their personal revolts, each argues for

117

a new order of reality, whether it be in rejecting the plans for the mental and social hygiene an institutional state would impose, or speaking out against the routine absurdity which through bureaucratic administration can come to pass as fact.

Both McMurphy and Yossarian become politicians in a larger sense, as culture heroes for the bold new decade of the American 1960s. Their creators, Ken Kesey and Joseph Heller, wrote outside of the literary establishment, and neither pursued the usual course of a "developing" author. *One Flew Over the Cuckoo's Nest* (New York: Viking, 1962) and *Catch-22* (New York: Simon and Schuster, 1961) are uniquely solitary works, far better known than their authors, and each serving as a talisman to the new culture. Standing alone because they anticipated (rather than continued) a tradition, they became known as underground novels, popularized and propagated by word-of-mouth recommendations quite independent of the establishment reviews and best-seller lists which continued to reflect the more closely drawn manners and morals (consider Saul Bellow, Bernard Malamud, John Updike) of the fifties. McMurphy and Yossarian were the first underground literary heroes of the new activist generation, proclaiming revolutionary new values which were as clear a signal as Kennedy's election that a new style and possibly a new reality were imminent.

One Flew Over the Cuckoo's Nest and *Catch-22* were first of all campus novels, and by the early 1960s academic conditions were such that a new market was available to insinuate these books into the consciousness of the youth culture, without using the traditional systems of distribution more likely to remain in conservative hands. The boom in higher education produced large classes of freshmen and sophomores, taught by a growing cadre of graduate assistants, and these books became two of the most widely taught novels in such circumstances. A decade earlier English classes were just discovering the great modernist works of the 1920s; but as the sixties dawned, literature suddenly became a pressing contemporary concern. Kesey and Heller spoke directly to young collegians, in terms they soon would echo in their own protests against society. McMurphy and Yossarian were initially presented as heroes by a young, newly (and even prematurely) enfranchised group of teachers as the first chosen models in a new educational situation. Such coincidence and reinforcement between methods and materials is one of the many reasons why the sixties, as a decade of change, made such an immediate impact.

JOINING FORCES: THE POLITICIAN AND THE DAYDREAMER

One Flew Over the Cuckoo's Nest speaks in the present tense, a signal of currency and of performance. The book *happens* like a movie. And it speaks directly to the reader, trusting the quality of *voice* to carry its effect far beyond the limited nature of its theme. "Who's the bull goose loony here?" shouts McMurphy as he bursts into the closely played world of the mental ward, its conformity and repression a perfect image of the fifties. What Mac says is important, but how he says it is what matters, embellishing his very presence with an aura of performance allusive to the wildness in America's past and the promise of her future:

> Then you tell Bull Goose Harding [the effeminate spokesman for the inmates] that R.P. McMurphy is waiting to see him and that this hospital ain't big enough for the two of us. I'm accustomed to being top man. I been a bull goose catskinner for every gyppo logging operation in the Northwest and bull goose gambler all the way from Korea, was even a bull goose pea weeder on that pea farm at Pendleton—so I figure if I'm bound to be a loony, then I'm bound to be a stompdown dadgum good one. Tell this Harding that he either meets me man to man or he's a yaller skunk and better be outta town by sunset.

The inmates realize at once that he is a politician, even a mythic one, incorporating aspects of the car salesman, stock auctioneer, and sideshow pitchman. McMurphy hits the ward like a bolt of summer lightning, not just for what he is in himself, but for what needs to be done in the hospital.

The hospital Mac has faked his way into is like none other in American fact or fiction. Phone wires whistle in the walls, electric current roars through conduits to appliances, fog machines deliberately obscure the grounds, and nuts-and-bolts technicians pull spare parts in and out of the patients at will. These images are metaphorical, at least to the reader. But to the novel's narrator, a Columbia River Indian named "Chief Broom" Bromden, they are strikingly real. Although officially described as a mental case, the Chief in fact suffers from (or enjoys the benefit of) a rich visual imagination. What may only be subtle intention on the part of the head nurse becomes in Bromden's mind a startling, physical actuality, and her manner of ward discipline is not only expressed by him in fantastic mechanical terms, but is extended to a larger vision of society, entirely restructured according to the nurse's ideal of absolute, repressive order.

Chief Bromden's mind resists the nurse's plan, and by playing deaf and dumb he is able to overhear what the other inmates miss. What the fifties called a disability, the sixties would redefine as great and touching eloquence. But his imagination has an even more important role in this novel. It is the fertile field on which McMurphy's ideas fall, the sensitive screen against which his flamboyant actions are played. If the Chief has expressed the imaginative truth of the nurse's repressive manner, he is also the one to mythologize McMurphy's resistance and rebellion. A hero such as Mac needs first of all to be perceived as a hero; and as our eyes and ears in this novel, the conventionally mute Chief Bromden becomes the expression of McMurphy's greatness.

A limited and closely defined set of images fills Chief Bromden's mind: the action among the ward's inmates, the Big Nurse's regimentation and more subtle manipulation of those inmates, the foreboding institutional and technological atmosphere (described as "operations of the Combine"), and McMurphy's posture in opposition to it all.

SPIRITUAL VERSUS MATERIAL PROGRESS

Mac is more vitally healthy than the pallid, insipid patients, for his own life of self-assertion is in direct contrast to the passive, depressive, and victimized stance inmates like Harding and Bibbit have taken toward the world. Because he has led the footloose life of a drifter, Mac has remained untouched by the Combine, which would use marriage and responsibility as pressures molding potential individuals into suburban ciphers, one interchangeable with another. *One Flew Over the Cuckoo's Nest* was one of the first novels to deal imaginatively with the hidden persuaders, the organization men, the lonely crowd, and other current sociological images of the fifties for a world of plenty the sixties generation would not worship but fear. Very shortly the age of affluence would be condemned as spiritually impoverished. The popularity of Chief Bromden's fears about the Combine is among the first signs of a change in cultural sentiment:

> The ward is a factory for the Combine. It's for fixing up mistakes made in the neighborhoods and in the schools and in the churches, the hospital is. When a completed product goes

back out into society, all fixed up good as new, *better* than new sometimes, it brings joy to the Big Nurse's heart; something that came in all twisted different is now a functioning, adjusted component, a credit to the whole outfit and a marvel to behold. Watch him sliding across the land with a welded grin, fitting into some nice little neighborhood where they're just now digging trenches along the street to lay pipes for city water. He's happy with it. He's adjusted to surroundings finally.

In the 1950s social conformity had been the ideal for material progress, and in the forties it was an even loftier virtue as part of the war effort. The new culture in the sixties questioned both, and Kesey emphasizes the fatal nature of "the Combine" by making its principal victim the Vanishing American who narrates this novel, a man who is being psy-

---

McMURPHY AND THE SEXUAL REVOLUTION

The 1960s brought a new openness about sexuality and an affirmation of it. Critic Robert Boyers finds this spirit of sexual revolution in One Flew Over the Cuckoo's Nest *disturbing.*

Kesey's solution to our common problem is the opening of floodgates, the releasing of energies which have too long lain unused or forgotten. Chief among these are the twin resources of laughter and uninhibited sexuality, the linkage between which Kesey manages to clarify in the course of his novel. . . .

[McMurphy] is something of a sensualist who dwells regularly on the ecstasies of sexual transport, and even goes so far as to bring his whores into the hospital to restore the vitality of his moribund fellow-psychopaths. . . .

At the heart of Kesey's notion of what is possible for modern liberated man is a phenomenon which one may call pornopolitics. . . .

It is in the spirit of random and thoroughly abandoned sexuality that Kesey's McMurphy would remake men, and subsequently the world. What is a little frightening in a novel like this, though, is that such a projection does not at all operate on a metaphorical level. Sex is not here a mere metaphor for passion, nor for any positive engagement with one's fellow human beings. There is a literalism in Kesey's suggestions of sexual apocalypse, with its unavoidable ramifications into a political and social context, which cannot be lightly taken.

Robert Boyers, "Attitudes Toward Sex in American 'High Culture,'" *Annals of the American Academy of Political and Social Sciences* (March 1968): 36–52.

chically destroyed by the same forces of social progress that killed his tribe.

Against these social forces, which by the 1960s had come to be perceived as threats, McMurphy places himself as a revolutionary hero. He is first of all a disruptionist, against the Big Nurse in particular and authority in general, and especially against the type of authority that inhibits self-expression and places limits on the individual. Like disruptionists of the coming decade, he sees that most of his acts must be theatrical, and much of his early effort is spent in gaming and baiting the Big Nurse. He challenges votes at her group meetings, smears her nurse's station window, disrupts her ward routine—all staged to the pleasure of the observing inmates. Even the pettiest acts are deliberately symbolic. They weaken the nurse, but more importantly they strengthen the men. Randall Patrick McMurphy is the first fictional hero to practice that key strategy of sixties leadership: *raising the consciousness of the people.* The ward inmates represent a cross section of American society, but his most responsive pupil is Chief Broom, a Native American, the First American, whom the progress of events has reduced to a deathlike silence. McMurphy restores the Chief to life, "blows him up whole again," and so reanimates America—just what the culturally regenerative movements of the sixties sought to do.

RENEWED LIFE: TURNING WEAKNESSES INTO STRENGTHS

McMurphy's role as animator is worth looking at more closely. Although the ward he checks into is physically and emotionally lifeless, its spirit broken by the strictures of the Big Nurse, McMurphy does not try to change any of its essential characteristics. Rather he transforms it into something positive. He does not deny that he and the others are "loonies," but rather asserts his looniness as part of the mechanics of greatness; he will become "bull goose loony" and offers the same potential to anyone else. Mad is beautiful, McMurphy preaches to these self-defeated patients who have let society's label destroy them. The therapies Mac develops do not contradict the inmates' condition, but rather exploit their so-called disabilities in order to create a new source of strength. One of the happiest moments in the ward (and one of the most enjoyably readable sections of the novel) is an interlude when the whole crew plays Monopoly, replete with bizarre rules and hallucinated playing pieces conceivable only in a madhouse. The equally improbable fishing trip lets every man play his own role to the fullest. McMurphy is truly a transformative hero. He changes the terms under which they are living, rather than changing their lives themselves. Laughter is his great weapon—"that big wide-open laugh of his. Dials twitch in the control panel at the sound of it." It is the one thing an otherwise totally helpless person can do, McMurphy teaches the men. And Chief Bromden remembers it as a weapon his father and other tribesmen used against the government. Though laughter is a physical expression, its substance is intellectual, even imaginative. In this way McMurphy is advocating a proletarian revolution of the mind; it is his new valuation of the terms of life which makes him a threat to the establishment. McMurphy is inventing a new way of perceiving reality, which is nothing less than a new reality itself.

The radical nature of McMurphy's challenge to the establishment is shown by the way the establishment strikes back. Emotional castration has kept the lesser inmates in line, but Mac's challenge has come from his imagination, and so castration of his mind—lobotomy—is the nurse's ultimate response. "I guess if she can't cut below the belt she'll do it above the eyes," Mac tells the Chief. For his part, Mac stays with the group and sacrifices himself for it—a new style of American heroism. The heroic tradition had been for a Natty Bumppo to strike off on his own, or for a Captain Ahab to sacrifice the group for his own ideal. "Anointest my head with conductant," Mac tells the electroshock therapist who begins his crucifixion, "Do I get a crown of thorns?" The Chief remarks several times how McMurphy has been weakened by his quest. As the men increase, Mac decreases, until by the end, when the inmates have taken control of their lives and the Chief has performed his superhuman act of throwing a hydrotherapy fount through the window and taking off for freedom, he is completely effaced from the novel. But only in body. The men walk with his swagger, boast with his bravado. McMurphy was the restorative spirit, and they have been restored.

A VIVID IMAGINATION

One Flew Over the Cuckoo's Nest presents a transformed vision of reality as well. And not just because the book's narrator has a richly imaginative way of perceiving things. Rather, that narrator has the special ability to play with the technical givens of his situation. He doesn't suffer from the mechanization of the Big Nurse's world; instead, he incorporates all its facets as elements of imaginative play, in a game he—not the nurse—controls. Even routine exposition benefits from this trick, making a richer, more imaginative, and ironically more personalized world to live in. "A tall bony old guy, dangling from a wire screwed in between his shoulder blades, met McMurphy and me at the door when the aides brought us in," the Chief narrates. "He looked us over with yellow, scaled eyes and shook his head. 'I wash my hands of the whole deal,' he told one of the colored aides, and the wire drug him off down the hall." The first characterization of the Big Nurse herself has been similarly composed of such native elements as the Chief finds handy for the art he can make from his world: "She slides through the door with a gust of cold and locks the door behind her and I see her fingers trail across the polished steel—tip of each finger the same color as her lips. Funny orange. Like the tip of a soldering iron." Throughout the novel Chief Bromden plays with his made-up images, his junk-sculpture from the manic-depressive ward. The nurse leaves a lipstick stain on a coffee cup, but the Chief believes "That color on the rim of the cup must be from heat, touch of her lips set it smoldering." The importance of the Chief's technique is obvious when we see the other typical activity of his mind: reconstructing idyllic memories of his young manhood on the Columbia River, before the government dispossessed his tribe. Both procedures are vital to his psychic health, as he refreshes himself in happy memories and actively works on the present to create a life of fiction. As the sixties developed, thinkers as various as psychiatrist R.D. Laing and philosopher Norman O. Brown would propose the same therapy to the culture at large.

But foremost is the way McMurphy, and especially the idea of McMurphy, operates on Chief Bromden's mind. Mac fills the Indian's imagination as the hero needed to revive him—"The iron in his boot heels crackled lightning out of the tile. He was the logger again, the swaggering gambler, the big redheaded Irishman, the cowboy out of the TV set walking down the middle of the street to meet a dare." As he has played with the mechanical image of the nurse, Chief Bromden embellishes the person of Randall McMurphy until it represents nearly every hero America has known for her mythic sustenance. For what he must do, McMurphy is made larger than life, too large even to be believable, just as the Chief's narration is too poetic to pass for day-to-day speech. "I been silent so long now," he tells us, "it's gonna roar out of me like floodwaters and you think the guy telling this is ranting and raving my *God*; you think this is too horrible to have really happened, this is too awful to be the truth!" Cultural conditions at the turn of the sixties demanded a prophet. "It's still hard for me to have a clear mind thinking on it," the Chief admits. "But it's the truth even if it didn't happen."...

RESISTING PREPACKAGED MARKETING

That movie audiences did not see adaptations of *One Flew Over the Cuckoo's Nest* and *Catch-22* until after the decade ended is even better proof that, as novels, they existed outside the pressure of commercial entertainment. If a book is successful as an economic investment, the film version usually comes a year later. Advertising, paperback publication, and film distribution reinforce each other in "tie-ins," and the product is marketed like an LP record—or, better yet, like a line of frozen pizzas. Under such conditions it is hard to tell whether the American public is responding to a deeply felt image in its developing culture, or whether it is being sold a bill of goods.

The movies from Kesey's and Heller's novels came much later, in the early 1970s. In their case a complementary principle of the American film industry was employed: if some films are made in response to commercial success, others try to manufacture a commercial success out of something already existing in the popular culture. Here the people supply the product to the industry, instead of the other way around. For nearly ten years McMurphy and Yossarian had helped express the redirection of a culture. They were popular far beyond the already large sales of their novels; their attitudes and beliefs pervaded American life, so that by the later 1960s they marched in the streets to protest similar institutional and bureaucratic monstrosities perpetrated by some who commanded our government. Davy Crockett, Daniel Boone, Paul Bunyan, and other such representative American characters were not created by a commercial entertainment complex, but their authentic popularity made them apt materials for commercial use. McMurphy and Yossarian described the new reality which underlay the politics of the 1960s, and the extent of their popularity, in their respective novels and films, flanks that decade almost as neatly as the numerological way we count off decades themselves.

McMurphy as Christ Figure

George N. Boyd

Beyond the political and social aspects of *Cuckoo's Nest*, the book operates on a Christian theological level through its symbolism and biblical references. Calling McMurphy a "secular Christ-figure," George N. Boyd, professor of religion at Trinity University in San Antonio, Texas, demonstrates how Kesey's plot and characters rely heavily on the traditional story of Jesus' martyrdom. McMurphy, like Jesus, heralds a new era at the hospital, bringing with him a message of goodness in the face of evil and hope in the face of hopelessness. His arrival brings with it a promise of spiritual renewal to his "disciples," the downtrodden inmates. McMurphy takes his disciples on a symbolic fishing trip, as well as succeeding in "healing" Chief Bromden, as Jesus healed those he touched. After struggles and persecution, McMurphy's lobotomy represents a crucifixion (on a cross-shaped table) by his tormentors (the Combine). Finally, McMurphy's sacrifice and martyrdom make him more powerful in death than in life. The parallels Boyd makes between McMurphy and Jesus, in spite of their obvious differences, are extraordinary.

The redemption in Kesey's story consists in the transformation of a group of mental asylum patients cowed by a tyrannical "Big Nurse" into men who begin to laugh, resist, and eventually try their own wings in launching themselves out of the oppressive security of the "Cuckoo's Nest." The agency of their liberation is the "contagious freedom"[1] of McMurphy, a boisterous, profane, fun-loving Irishman who has

---

1. I am borrowing here the term used by Paul Van Buren to describe the redemptive quality of Jesus. See *The Secular Meaning of the Gospel* (New York: Macmillan, 1963), p. 133.

Excerpted from George N. Boyd, "Parables of Costly Grace: Flannery O'Connor and Ken Kesey," *Theology Today*, vol. 29, no. 3 (1972), pp. 161–71. Reprinted with permission of *Theology Today*.

feigned psychosis in order to trade a six-month work farm sentence for what he has assumed to be the softer life of an asylum. Waging a hilarious guerrilla campaign, McMurphy mocks, ignores, and evades the petty restrictions of Miss Ratched's authoritarian order. He unsettles her smooth rule and brings a spark of humor and hope to the men, but until his climactic self-sacrifice, he can ignite only feeble and sporadic imitation.

Superficially *Cuckoo's Nest* is a parable of resistance to a dehumanizing techno-bureaucratic society. As seen by the narrator, Chief Broom, the asylum is society in microcosm; Miss Ratched is the agent of the "Combine," the name for all institutions and powers which prefer to keep men docile and conformist. According to Harding, the most articulate of McMurphy's companions, the men are rabbits, although what puts them in the asylum is not the rabbithood they share with men generally, but rather their inability to "accommodate" themselves to their rabbithood. "Cure" consists in "adjustment"—adjustment to the authoritarian conventions which are upheld by a firm if subtle compulsion aided by the individual's anxiety-rooted tendency toward conformity.

Perhaps the most demonic aspect of the adjustment process (and, by implication, also of the society for which the asylum is the factory for retooling misfitting parts) is the pseudo-democratic group meeting in which the patients are made the agents of their own emasculation. While theoretically they can establish many of their own rules (the TV hours, cigarette consumption, etc.), they are subject to various forms of administrative retribution if they resist the suggestions and preferences of those with power over them. In one incident, the men failed to support McMurphy's motion to adjust the TV hours during the World Series, and after they were shamed into support, the set was disconnected. Sporadically, McMurphy brings some substance into this formal but illusory democracy, but of course even this involves no choice concerning the basic direction of the institution.

THE GOSPEL ACCORDING TO KESEY

Such an interpretation is accurate enough as far as it goes, but as long as McMurphy himself sees the contest only in this perspective, he is rather easily beaten. After his initial victory in momentarily breaking Miss Ratched's icy composure, he becomes a model patient. With some bitterness that his friends had not better informed him, he explains his reformed behavior as stemming from the discovery that his commitment is indefinite, rather than only for the remainder of his six-month prison term, and that discharge depends on the favor of the nurse. Realizing why they submit, he'll do the same, since he has as much to lose as any of them, but then McMurphy is shocked with the news that he has much more than they to lose. Most of the others are "voluntary" rather than "committed" and cannot be held without their consent. The problem is not merely the "combine"; it is, more deeply, their own lack of will. For once McMurphy is speechless, but the next day his resistance resumes, no longer as a game but as a struggle to the death which finally elicits a corresponding response from his fellow inmates.[2]

Again expressed in theological terminology, McMurphy's "contagious freedom" is finally effective when he becomes quite literally "a man for others,"[3] living out a voluntary mission of redemptive suffering. Kesey obviously intends McMurphy to be a secular Christ-figure. At the most explicit level of symbolism, McMurphy's defiance leads him to a series of shock treatments on a table "shaped like a cross." McMurphy refused the customary sedation (pills instead of drugged wine—cf. Mark 15:23), joked about their "anointing" his head with conductant, and requested a crown of thorns which he got in the form of a crown of sparks. Still not broken after repeated treatments but beginning to be threatened with a lobotomy, McMurphy's friends urge him to escape, but he insists on staying in order to give mother-dominated Billy his first experience of "manhood." When they are caught the next morning because all the disciples and, in this case, the Messiah as well, had fallen asleep, he is betrayed by a disciple. Billy, unable to bear the nurse's threat to tell his mother, breaks down, puts all the blame on McMurphy, and then to complete his Judas role, cuts his own throat. The nurse charges McMurphy with playing with the lives of men "as if you thought yourself to be a god." Breaking the detailed passion parallel, McMurphy tears off

2. Joseph J. Waldmeir, in nearly the only exception to the critical black-out, confuses the structure of the story by missing this crucial transformation and seeing a gradual expansion of McMurphy's motivation. "Two Novelists of the Absurd: Heller and Kesey," *Contemporary Literature*, V (Autumn, 1964), No. 3, 200. 3. This phrase, originating in Bonhoeffer's "Outline for a Book," probably comes closer than any other to representing a summary Christology among radical theologians. Dietrich Bonhoeffer, *Letters and Papers from Prison*, Third Edition, edited by Eberhard Bethge (New York: Macmillan, 1967), p. 210.

her clothes and chokes her until subdued by attendants, but, at the end of the struggle, "he lets himself cry out" "when he finally doesn't care anymore about anything but himself and his dying."

As with Jesus, McMurphy's influence on his disciples is stronger in his absence than in his presence. Unless he goes away, his spirit of freedom will not come to be theirs as well (cf. John 6:7), and they will remain dependent. Indeed they cannot think of him as absent—his "*presence* still tramping up and down the halls and laughing out loud in the meetings and singing in the latrines," precludes the nurse's attempt to re-establish the old era in the ward. In the following days, all but one of the non-committed patients leave or transfer wards, and even the weak doctor, the Pilate who in hand-washing fashion signs all the papers as the politically influential nurse bids him, becomes his own man. When the lobotomized McMurphy is brought back to the ward as a vegetable, his remaining disciples first deny that this body could be the real McMurphy; and then, in effect, they hide the body (cf. Matthew 28:13) so that it cannot be displayed as a token of the effects of bucking the system. Chief Broom, the narrator of the story, a huge Indian who for years has feigned deafness and dumbness until McMurphy saw through him and restored him to human communication (for how could McMurphy be the Messiah if he didn't make the deaf hear and the dumb speak), suffocates McMurphy in his sleep. Chief Broom then flees the Cuckoo's Nest with the help of a companion who assists in bringing "to remembrance" (cf. John 14:26) the things McMurphy had taught them ("He showed you how one time. . . . You remember"). The Chief's flight concludes the resurrection experiences, and Kesey's gospel ends.

McMurphy the Messiah

With growing risk of interpretive excess, the Christ-figure details can be expanded indefinitely. In analogy with Jesus (cf. John 6:16–21), the high point in McMurphy's career is marked by his wheedling permission to take twelve of them on a day's fishing excursion; at least one fish is almost too heavy to bring into the boat; the weather worsens but narrowly they get safely back. Yet immediately afterwards (cf. John 6:66), the disciples (in this case including the twelve) begin to fall away, yielding to the nurse's suggestion that Mc-

---

BIBLICAL ECHOES IN *CUCKOO'S NEST*

In elaborating the comparisons between McMurphy and Jesus, George N. Boyd cites nine specific passages from the Gospels of the New Testament. The following biblical excerpts are taken from these passages.

And they offered him wine mingled with myrrh; but he did not take it.

And Jesus cried again with a loud voice and yielded up his spirit.

And Jesus uttered a loud cry, and breathed his last.

Nevertheless I tell you the truth: it is to your advantage that I go away, for if I do not go away, the Counselor will not come to you; but if I go, I will send him to you.

"Tell people, 'His disciples came by night and stole him away while we were asleep.'. . ."

But the Counselor, the Holy Spirit, whom the Father will send in my name, he will teach you all things, and bring to your remembrance all that I have said to you.

When evening came, his disciples went down to the sea, got into a boat, and started across the sea to Capernaum. It was now dark, and Jesus had not yet come to them. The sea rose because a strong wind was blowing. When they had rowed about three or four miles, they saw Jesus walking on the sea and drawing near to the boat. They were frightened, but he said to them, "It is I; do not be afraid." Then they were glad to take him into the boat, and immediately the boat was at the land to which they were going.

After this many of his disciples drew back and no longer went about with him.

And he said, "Ab'ba, Father, all things are possible to thee; remove this cup from me; yet not what I will, but what thou wilt."

The Holy Bible, Revised Standard Edition containing the Old and New Testaments. New York: Penguin Books, 1962.

Murphy is only staying around for the money he wins off them in various and slightly deceptive gambling schemes. Joseph Waldmeir, who otherwise notes only the most explicit Christ symbolism (the electro-therapy sequence), suggests that the Chief in strangling McMurphy represents McMurphy's priest offering and partaking of the sacrifice of the already dead victor-victim in order to be renewed by his life.[4]

Whatever the reason for the detailed Christ-figure, *Cuckoo's Nest* is not deliberately a parable for secular Chris-

4. Waldmeir, *op. cit.,* p. 203.

tianity, certainly not in the sense of being an illustration of anyone's theological viewpoint. At the time of its publication in 1962, the death-of-God theology was merely in its late gestation stage. Tom Wolfe's account of Kesey's role as prophet-messiah of the Merry Pranksters quotes Kesey as saying that despite the Pranksters' increasingly religious interpretation of their psychedelic life, it is not the "Christ-trip . . . that's been done . . . and then you have 2000 years of war."[5] Nevertheless, McMurphy is a model of a "contagiously free" "man for others." As Chief Broom realizes:

> It was us that had been making him go on for weeks, keeping him standing long after his feet and legs had given out, weeks of making him wink and grin and laugh and go on with his act long after his humor had been parched dry between two electrodes (pp. 304–305).

Though McMurphy wants to free himself to live on his own terms (cf. Mark 14:36), he cannot since "he had signed on for the whole game."

Yet "man for others" is a terribly inadequate summary phrase for McMurphy and an equally unfortunate one for Jesus as well. In each case one has the story of a man who is faithful to his own sense of identity and who insists on maintaining it at whatever cost. Both intend their lifestyles as models of authentic humanity for their friends; they even sacrifice themselves to that sense of mission; and the desire not to betray those others reinforces their determination in the face of temptation to find an easy way out. However, none of this alters their fundamental commitments to be whatever they understood themselves to be. In a description of McMurphy's motivation which can be applied to Jesus as well, Waldmeir says that for Billy's death to be meaningful "McMurphy must win, must be free, must live; but in order to win he must lose, in order to be free he must bind himself inextricably, in order to live he must be destroyed. The only alternative is to desert the struggle."[6]

Both McMurphy and Jesus conform to the expectations of their friends as little as they do to those of the authorities, and they remain self-centered enough to make a few somewhat deceptive gambling dollars or accept the costly ointment which could buy food for the poor. A man who is only "for others" would be so devoid of human personality that

5. Tom Wolfe, *The Electric Kool-Aid Acid Test* (New York: Farrar, Strauss, and Giroux, Inc., 1968), p. 193. 6. Waldmeir, *op. cit.*, p. 202.

his sacrifice of "self" would be empty and his presence boring; surely [psychologist] Erich Fromm is right that one who does not love himself cannot genuinely love others. Bonhoeffer himself was aware of this. In his letter of May 6, 1944, he promised that "I shall be writing next time about Christians' 'egotism' (selfless self-love). . . . Too much altruism is oppressive."[7] Unfortunately the promise was forgotten, and this passage has not qualified the excesses in the usage of "the man for others" phrase.

THE STRUGGLE CONTINUES

There is, of course, no once-for-all atonement in McMurphy's struggle: ". . . the thing he was fighting, you couldn't whip it for good. All you could do was keep on whipping it, till you couldn't come out any more and somebody else had to take your place." What Kesey has given us is an affirmation of spontaneity, love, life, and freedom over conformity, docility, and death. He offers the declaration that although such a style may have a cross as its price tag, crosses can be redemptive and resurrection may have the last word. McMurphy is resurrected in the lives of his disciples. Of course, this does not eliminate the personal loss for the man who relishes the life he surrenders to those who secretly hate life, nor the public loss of the good incarnate wherever life is lived with such relish.

7. Bonhoeffer, *op. cit.*, pp. 157–158 (Letter of May 6, 1944).

McMurphy as Tragic Hero

Michael M. Boardman

Cuckoo's Nest is a tragedy in that McMurphy brings
about his own destruction through his commitment to
save the inmates. Because self-destruction seems unre-
alistic for a character whose instinct for survival is so
well developed, Kesey makes use of literary devices to
bring about his plot.

According to Michael M. Boardman, professor of English
at Tulane University at the time this article was published,
one such device is the first-person narrator, in this case Chief
Bromden. As narrator, the Chief influences the reader to see
McMurphy's fall as tragic because his own freedom is dependent on McMurphy's death. Since we are sympathetic to this
narrator, we are eager for McMurphy to act in his behalf. Another device Kesey uses is the protagonist's changing outlook
during the course of the novel—the character grows and develops and therefore views his own life differently by the end
of the book.

Boardman points to criticism of Kesey's religious comparisons as being far-fetched and contrived. Likewise, many
have felt that Kesey has unnecessarily demeaned women in
his efforts to move his plot along by making Big Nurse such a
total embodiment of evil.

Ultimately, says Boardman, the tragedy in *Cuckoo's Nest*
lies not in McMurphy's lobotomy and death, but rather in the
loss of his individuality. This loss of self gradually comes
about as his actions become more and more controlled by
the expectations and needs of others.

When McMurphy enters the hateful world of the Big Nurse,
he reminds the narrator, Chief Bromden, "of a car salesman
or a stock auctioneer," hardly a candidate for martyrdom.
No one can "tell if he's really this friendly or if he's got some
gambler's reason for trying to get acquainted with guys so

Excerpted from Michael M. Boardman, "*One Flew Over the Cuckoo's Nest:* Rhetoric and
Vision," *Journal of Narrative Technique,* vol. 9, no. 3 (1979), pp. 171–83. Reprinted with
permission from the *Journal of Narrative Technique.*

far gone a lot of them don't even know their names." Against this long-developed instinct for survival wars a common human concern his independence has not extirpated: will he act to help the men or to help himself? At first, he bets he can "bug" the "Big Nurse," a sexually repressed and supremely efficient force for conformity who has learned to "smell out" the fear of her patients and "put it to use." In numerous important scenes, we learn the extent of her power to prevent noisome independence: she can, in addition to all the little arts of prodding the guilty recesses of her "patients'" consciences, order electric shock, even lobotomize the recalcitrant or merely disruptive patient. The connection between Mac's behaving himself, playing it "cagey," and staying in one piece becomes clear to us and to him when, after promising to "bug" the nurse "till she comes apart at those neat little seams," he learns that he can be institutionalized as long as the nurse sees fit. He immediately becomes cagey, satisfying, temporarily at least, the Chief's earlier question about his motivation: Mac is for Mac. He has had "no one to *care* about, which is what makes him free enough to be a good con man," and the first duty of a con artist is survival. The terms of the action are set. If he acts to defy the nurse, he risks destruction, past reminders of which, the "Vegetables," are conveniently and conspicuously placed around the ward. If he plays it cagey, as all his past experience has taught him to do, not only will he be safe but eventually free.

HOW TO DESTROY A SURVIVALIST

Kesey's problem with this pattern should be apparent. How could he show McMurphy acting, in a manner entirely out of character, to insure his own destruction? In addition, even if Kesey could find a plausible way to motivate McMurphy's sacrifice, how, given the power of the combine and Nurse Ratched, could the horror of senseless waste be avoided? . . .

But Kesey's problem was more than just persuasion. Not only was McMurphy to give his life away; he was to do so in conflict against a microcosmic representation of a brutal and unforgiving society that valued his independence not at all. The potential for horror was great. Kesey's solution was to create not only a first-person narrator, but one whose entire well being depended on the sacrifice toward which McMurphy gradually moved. The Chief's "fog" is the sign that McMurphy is playing it cagey; for the reader, it is the signal to regret Mac's caution and desire his continued resistance to the Big Nurse, even though we may care greatly for him and fear his peril. When everything seems "hopeless and dead," when the Chief feels "McMurphy can't help. . . . Nobody can help," that is when "the fog rolls in." Kesey carefully handles the relationship between Mac's attitude toward the hospital and the nurse, and the Chief's mental health. Very quickly, one implies the other with almost syllogistic force.

As Mac inches toward destruction—it is never really in doubt, once we have seen the past and present power of the Big Nurse—a corresponding reduction in the Chief's psychosis takes place. The other inmates are part of the immanent and powerful pattern, showing clear signs of independence, sexual and otherwise. It is as if the entire cast of characters supporting Mac and the Big Nurse has been invented to convert an implausible and horrifying tale into one that is inevitable and transcending. There should be no confusion over just who this story is "about." For all of the Chief's importance and vividness as a narrator, he is still part of the "telling" and not the "essence." Aside from being one of the strangest "reliable" narrators in fiction, the Chief provides the compelling need that, coupled with that of the other men, drives Mac on. . . .

The Chief's desires, and those of the other men, would not be enough to establish the instability that leads, in a series of gradually more direct acts of rebellion, to Mac's lobotomy and death. Even with "every one of those faces" on the Disturbed Ward "turned toward him" and "waiting" for him to act, something in Mac's personality must make the confrontation inevitable. Here is where Kesey had perhaps his trickiest problem. If the battle were simply between the Nurse's absolute desire for control and Mac's con man independence, we have melodrama. What Kesey does instead is to represent, largely from the outside, through the perceptions of the Chief, a change in Mac. The tragic fate he endures—distinct from the lobotomy and death that are its effects—is to lose his personality in the other men. The McMurphy who leads his twelve disciples down to the sea to fish for salmon has relinquished his role as dynamic and independent rabblerouser. On the trip back, with seas high, he takes a life-jacket, even though they were three short. The old Mac would have played the tough leader, disdaining the whipping waves. But now, "McMurphy hadn't insisted that he be one of the heroes; all during the fuss he'd stood with his back against the cabin . . . and watched the guys without saying a word," a reticence equally unusual for Mac. Harding, near the end, sees the change clearly. It hasn't been the nurse "bugging" Mac "about one thing or another." "That's not what drove you crazy," Harding says. It was "us," the men who turned the independence of Mac into the only kind of weakness that could have destroyed him: the ability to care about others.

Kesey risked creating a mere comic book hero in Mac, a caricature of real heroism. We do not see the psychological process that turns Mac from egocentric sinner to sacrificial saint; it is portrayed through signs: Mac's uneasiness, noted by the Chief, his "dreadfully tired and strained and *frantic*" look as he realizes, we surmise, what he must do. . . .

CRITICISM OF KESEY'S METHODS

Some readers find the comparisons of Mac to Christ not only heavy-handed but inappropriate. But this too is a rhetorical problem: to elevate Mac's actions to tragic proportions, not only must a great deal be at stake (the other men) but his struggle must seem larger than it objectively is. Kesey may intend a "statement" about the "Combine," the American society with its passion for homogenization; but that "lesson" is present only indirectly as a function of Kesey's need to raise the confrontation above the level of local melodrama. . . .

Many other elements of the novel function as rhetoric to establish the importance of McMurphy's fall, including the sense that it is not merely idiosyncratic, but somehow "true," universal in its implications and importance. Here is where Kesey has run into the most trouble with critics and general readers. . . . The Big Nurse, for example, has been seen as evidence of Kesey's "demeaning" attitude toward women, a charge that could be brought against Shakespeare because he created Lady Macbeth. For the dramatic requirements of the story, Nurse Ratched had to be very nearly an incarnation of evil, unthinking or otherwise. For Mac's struggle to seem important, the forces opposing him must not only seem nearly omnipotent, but must not be too "understandable," and never sympathetic. Here is one place, among many, where [*Cuckoo's Nest* film director] Milos Forman, and laudatory critics of the movie version, seem to me

KESEY'S McMURPHY AND MELVILLE'S AHAB: TWO TRAGIC HEROES

In delineating the comparisons between McMurphy and Captain Ahab, the protagonist in Herman Melville's Moby-Dick, *critic Edward Stone suggests the basic characteristics of the tragic hero, who goes forward charismatically in a battle he must lose.*

The stranger who dominates Kesey's insane-asylum stage from the moment he appears reveals outlandish underpants given to him, McMurphy explains, by a literature major at a state university " 'because she said I was a symbol.' " Since the black satin shorts are covered with big white whales (with red eyes), the symbolism in question may have been Herman Melville's. Actually, there is a great measure of the appropriate in the student's interpretation of the maniacal Randle P. McMurphy. We notice that the most pronounced of Mac's physical features is the new scar on his nose, reminiscent of the scar running down Ahab's face, and that his latest and fatal adversary is encased in white. Mac's brawling vitality that refuses to yield to the insuperable authority of Big Nurse parallels Ahab's fierce refusal to submit to the tyranny of the gods, and his final assault on her is just as inevitable and as suicidal. Like the White Whale, Big Nurse herself is a symbol: the one, of the evil in the world and the other, of the repression of the vital sex force. Like Ishmael, Chief Bromden, Kesey's narrator, emerges, chastened, to tell the story . . . to observe [McMurphy's] "humanities," to share his confidences with the reader, to describe his ability to bend the other patients to his wishes and his inability to heed their warnings about his nemesis's power.

Edward Stone, "Straws for the Cuckoo's Nest," *Journal of Popular Culture* 10.1 (1976): 199–202.

to have gone completely astray. The last thing Kesey needed was a "humanized portrait of Big Nurse," one that would make "viewers wish to know more about the character."[1] . . . To criticize Kesey for not showing how the Big Nurse got to be a "bitch" is to forget that she is not a real person but a character subordinated to the realization of a tragic plot. A little understanding, where villains are concerned, often courts artistic disaster; with the Big Nurse, as with [Shakespeare's] Iago, the moral terms of the struggle need to be clear in order to prevent confusion. . . .

1. Marsha McCreadie, *"One Flew Over the Cuckoo's Nest:* Some Reasons for One Happy Adaptation," *Literature/Film Quarterly* 5 (1977): 130.

THE TRAGEDY IS NOT DEATH, BUT LOSS OF INDIVIDUALITY

McMurphy's fate is indeed to become the kind of "savior" he scorns being treated as earlier in the novel. All of the rhetoric of the book is designed to make plausible his final attack on the nurse, an act he cannot avoid, that will destroy him, and yet one that is out of character for the "cagey" Mac. Like most tragic figures, Mac's physical destruction is not identical to his doom. His tragic fate is to become fatally dependent on the men, to act in a way that makes clear that he is under the control of their needs and desires. What removes the "conversion" of Mac from the merely melodramatic is that he loses himself largely without recognizing— at least, so that *we* can see it—what is happening. Harding, usually a perceptive witness, errs for once when he argues, after the fishing trip, that "everything he's done was done with reason." We have seen no process of ratiocination indicating a calculated intention. In fact, at crucial points in the book, when Mac must take another rebellious step closer to lobotomy, what we see is a man who would avoid the confrontation if he could. In the shower room scene, Mac finally makes himself fight only when it is clear that Washington will not leave the men alone, will insist on soaping down the frantic and helpless George. McMurphy reacts, with "helpless, cornered despair" in his voice By keeping the thoughts of McMurphy hidden, by indicating his state of mind through signs the Chief interprets, Kesey manages simultaneously to achieve two difficult ends: we do not question the plausibility of Mac's actions, and we desire more and more that he continue them. Our fears for him are not allowed enough strength to conquer our stronger desires that he act to help the men. It is as if Kesey had discovered that a powerful tragic action could be constructed around the spectacle of a man who is destroyed because he is forced to become better than he was. All the authorial rhetoric at Kesey's command, including the hiding of certain things, had to be employed to prevent such a character from seeming merely pitiful or his destruction evidence of the multifarious horror of existence. . . .

SEEING THROUGH THE CHIEF'S EYES

It is tempting to accept Kesey's own appraisal of his subject, to concur with his often quoted statement that "It's the Indian's story—not McMurphy's or Jack Nicholson's." But Kesey goes on, immediately, to suggest,what I think is the real conception underlying the novel: "The emphasis should . . . be . . . on the battle going on in the Indian's mind between this man and the Combine that is loose in America."[2] The Chief, that is, controls our responses to the conflict by himself responding in ways that compel us to wish for McMurphy to act. . . . I have tried to demonstrate that when we ask, of Bromden's role as narrator, "for the sake of what," the answer is clearly to tell McMurphy's story as powerfully as possible. At any point in the novel, our fear or happiness for the Chief results almost entirely from how he views McMurphy.

The tragic conception, then, rests on McMurphy. Kesey is correct, in addition, to suggest that the conflict is between Mac and the Combine. The Big Nurse is a representative. But what gives the book its tragic power, what assimilates it to the great tragedies of all ages, is that the conflict is never merely *between* figures but leads to an internal struggle, mirrored at every point by the Chief's responses. Despite the vast dissimilarities between Kesey's novel and many of Shakespeare's tragedies, there are yet these two important similarities. The struggle with Nurse Ratched and the Combine becomes, inside McMurphy, a fight between two opposed principles of his being. Like Hamlet, McMurphy must become something other than what he was for the disaster— and the victory that accompanies high tragedy—to take place; and like many of Shakespeare's tragic heroes, McMurphy finds himself in a situation in which the ethically "correct" choice—although it will doom him—is one for which none of his previous experiences has prepared him. When faced with the chance to escape at the end of the novel, he calmly turns the opportunity down: "I've took their best punch." Harding realizes that Mac does not "fully comprehend" what can happen to him. But the Chief has already told us that "it was bound to be and would have happened in one way or another . . . there wasn't any way of him breaking his contract." The "bull goose loony" has become loony indeed; he can no longer care only for his own survival.

2. Ken Kesey, in Beverly Grunwald, "Kesey: A Sane View from 'Cuckoo's Nest,'" *Women's Wear Daily*, December 18, 1975, p. 1.

McMurphy's Evolution

Richard Blessing

McMurphy's initials, RPM, suggest that he is the per-
sonification of motion, energy, and change. A drifter
with a short attention span, he has managed to evade
the Combine through constant movement, because, as
Chief Bromden says, "a moving target is hard to hit."
Recognizing in McMurphy the classic American hero,
readers see him in turn as frontiersman, con man, father, martyr, and god.

So what becomes of the speed-oriented McMurphy when he is caught, caged, and made to sit still?
Richard Blessing, English professor at the University
of Washington, discusses the ways in which he finds
other outlets for his pent-up energy. McMurphy discovers that if he can't engage in *physical* movement,
then he must engage in *mental* movement. This mental energy is put to use against the cold, mechanical
Combine—as represented by Big Nurse and the institution—when he tries to free the inmates and thwart
the system. Blessing writes that in doing so, while Mc-
Murphy does not bodily leave the hospital, he moves
in the spiritual direction of love.

This RPM principle of motion and change, as em-
bodied by McMurphy, represents freedom from confinement of all kinds—or the triumph of the individual spirit.

McMurphy, as his initials suggest, is the embodiment of motion and consequently, if life is motion, an embodiment of
the life force as well. Chief Bromden, the Indian narrator
who promises that all he tells us is "the truth even if it didn't
happen," reasons that it is speedy and continuous movement
that has kept McMurphy free to be his own man.

Maybe he growed up so wild all over the country, batting
around from one place to another, never around one town

Excerpted from Richard Blessing, "The Moving Target: Ken Kesey's Evolving Hero,"
Journal of Popular Culture, vol. 4, no. 3 (1971), pp. 615–27. Reprinted by permission of
Popular Press.

longer'n a few months when he was a kid so a school never
got much hold on him, logging, gambling, running carnival
wheels, travelling light-footed and fast, keeping on the move
so much that the Combine never had a chance to get anything
installed. Maybe that's it, he never gave the Combine a
chance. . . because a moving target is hard to hit.

Even when restrained by the walls of the hospital, Mc-
Murphy is characterized by energy. Kesey associates his
hero with rapid and relentless motion and stresses his ability to be the cause of movement in others. When McMurphy
first arrives on the ward, the black boys find it impossible to
get him to hold still long enough to hit the target with a rec-
tal thermometer. The songs he habitually sings, "The Roving
Gambler" and "The Wagoner's Lad," are songs in which the
protagonist is a wanderer, a "mover" who is hard to pin
down, even when a good woman does her best. As a basketball coach, McMurphy specializes in the fast break ("Drive,
you puny mothers, *drive!*") and has his charges zooming
from one end of the ward to the other in helter-skelter lack
of formation. . . .

One of the vital triumphs of freedom and motion over
confinement and fixity is, of course, the fishing trip pro-
moted by McMurphy. . . . Nevertheless, the "government
sponsored expedition" must sign in as it had signed out, and
the men must return to the asylum of the Big Nurse.

OUTRUNNING BIG NURSE

It is there, on Miss Ratched's territory, that McMurphy is
compelled to carry on the struggle. All physical advantages
are hers. Cement walls, iron doors, strait jackets, tranquil-
lizing drugs and almost unbreakable screens combine to arrest movement before it becomes a serious threat to the
good, static and ordered way of things. And so it is that Mc-
Murphy, who has always kept himself free of the "Combine"
by "batting around from one place to another," must find a
way to translate ordinary physical growth and movement
into the dimensions of the spirit, mind and heart. Confined
to the ward, McMurphy must substitute an evolution in
character for his customary speed of foot.

Of course, changes in the spirit, mind and heart may be
made mechanically as well as organically. It is mechanistic
change that is the Big Nurse's ultimate weapon. A man may
be altered by giving him Electro Shock Therapy or by a lo-

botomy, and in either case the intention is to create a smoothly shaped part to fit the social machine. "A successful Dismissal . . . is a product that brings joy to the Big Nurse's heart and speaks good of her craft and the whole industry in general." Such "products" are manufactured, not grown or developed. Maxwell Taber, for example, takes on an entirely new personality after his lobotomy.

> Why, I've never seen anything to beat the change in Maxwell Taber since he's got back from the hospital; a little black and blue around the eyes, a little weight lost, and, you know what? he's a *new man.* Gad, modern American science.

On the other hand, McMurphy's spiritual evolution is an organic process in which nothing of what he is becomes totally lost. The qualities that he brings onto the ward are still with him when he departs to his lobotomy, but many of them have developed and changed almost beyond recognition. The McMurphy who goes to his mechanized martyrdom is at once the shaggy rebel who first enters the ward and an apotheosized figure almost noble enough to be a full, perfect and sufficient sacrifice for the sins and weaknesses of the entire ward. . . .

The Quintessential American Hero

When the reader first meets McMurphy, Kesey's protagonist seems very familiar indeed. In fact, the early McMurphy can be seen as a conglomerate hero made up of archetypal figures common to American folk, popular and classical cultures—figures known by even the least literate of television gazers.

Essentially, the McMurphy who enters the ward is a frontier hero, an anachronistic paragon of rugged individualism, relentless energy, capitalistic shrewdness, virile coarseness and productive strength. . . . He is the descendant of the pioneer who continually fled civilization and its feminizing and gentling influence. He has managed to live with "No wife wanting new lineoleum. No relatives pulling at him with watery old eyes. No one to *care* about, which is what makes him free. . . ." Like all successful frontiersmen, those dwellers on the cutting edge of civilization where the law affords no protection from the vicious who would live by the gun or the fist, McMurphy is a good fighter. He is the "big redheaded brawling Irishman," one of a robust breed. . . .

Closely allied to McMurphy's fighting skill is his ability to do work, to use his power to subdue nature to useful ends.

Kesey makes him a logger, a "bull goose catskinner for every gyppo logging operation in the Northwest." McMurphy is also associated with that other hardworking masculinity figure of American culture, the cowboy. . . . The images of logger and cowboy alternate and combine, reminding the reader of McMurphy's kinship with Paul Bunyan and Pecos Bill; with the "logger lover" who, according to the ballad, stirred his coffee with his thumb and the Lone Ranger; and with Jason Bolt of "Here Come the Brides" and the Marlboro man of television and magazine advertising.

Another archetypal American hero is the gambler, the hustler, the confidence man. And McMurphy is one of the finest specimens of the breed. . . . Of course, Americans have always loved shrewd operators, even while being "taken" by them. From P.T. Barnum to . . . Lyndon Johnson, the "wheeler-dealer" is admired and respected as a kind of off-shoot of the "clever hero" of folklore.[1] Thus, Harding probably speaks for most Americans when he defends McMurphy's character.

> He has a healthy and honest attitude about his chicanery, and I'm all for him, just as I'm for the dear old capitalistic system of free individual enterprise, comrades, for him and his downright bullheaded gall and the American flag, bless it, and the Lincoln Memorial and the whole bit. Remember the Maine, P.T. Barnum and the Fourth of July. I feel *compelled* to defend my friend's honor as a good old red, white and blue hundred-per-cent American con man.

It is one of his gambler's skills that begins to lead McMurphy to his compassion for the inmates of the ward. "The secret of being a top-notch con man," he says, "is being able to know what the mark wants. . . . You fe-e-el the sucker over with your eyes when he comes up and you say, 'Now here's a bird that needs to feel tough.'" The knowledge of human nature that tells the gambler what his victim needs to feel is a knowledge that can, if he is not careful, grow into empathy and then into love itself. . . .

CON MAN OUTCONNED?

So McMurphy is the mirror of the classic patterns of American manhood. And that is not enough. Confronted by a force that he can't outrun, outwit, outlast, con, slug, seduce or rape, he is thoroughly baffled for some time. His bewilderment is, I suppose, that of the frontiersman of dynamic and organic values who finds himself in a world which rewards only the mechanistic and antiseptic in human life. If he is to win his battle with the Big Nurse, he must grow beyond the McMurphy who enters the hospital.

The silly wager that McMurphy makes quickly becomes a struggle for the hearts, minds and genitals of the inmates of the ward. In order to win, McMurphy must come to see himself as the men see him and, harder still, he must accept the responsibility of *being* what they need him to be. He must, in short, *become* the symbol that the Oregon co-ed had in mind when she gave him his Moby Dick shorts; he must *become* the Chief's "giant come out of the sky to save us from the Combine. . . ." He must become a different, larger sort of archetype, a fertility god or a primitive father-figure capable of guiding into manhood the "boys" who live under the matriarchy of the Big Nurse. . . .

MOTION THROUGH DEATH

As phallic father, McMurphy finds that his sons unconsciously become his enemies. They drain him of energy, tie him down, betray him and finally murder him. But only by his sacrifice can they become men. The death of fathers thrusts sons into manhood, ready or not, and so it is with the death of McMurphy.

> Everything was changing. Sefelt and Frederickson signed out together Against Medical Advice, and two days later another three Acutes left, and six more transferred to another ward. . . . [T]he doctor was informed that his resignation would be accepted and he informed them that they would have to go the whole way and can him if they wanted him out.

For a time, it seems that McMurphy can restore life to the ward wasteland without losing his own life, but as he grows more and more aware of the greatness of the need of the men who surround him, he also becomes more aware of the cost of fulfilling that need. The Indian reads in McMurphy's face in a windshield the strain and fatigue of trying to save the inmates in the little time he has left. And the Indian knows that

> [W]e were the ones making him do it. . . . It was us that had been making him go on for weeks, keeping him standing long after his feet and legs had given out, weeks of making him wink and grin and laugh and go on with his act long after his humor had been parched dry between two electrodes.

Now this is love; there is no other name for it. The gambler's shrewd sense of what the mark needs to feel has become the father's desire to fulfill that need. And that desire has, in turn, become transformed into the highest kind of human love, the love that will lay down its life for another. . . .

So it is that McMurphy—American folk hero, fertility god and primitive father, Christ figure—wins even as he loses. His values—courage, strength, manliness, pride, compassion and self-sacrifice—triumph over the de-humanizing values of the plastic society that destroys his body. He has kept moving, even when confined by a strait jacket. And from him we can learn to be moving targets, bobbing and weaving as we approach the twenty-first century.

NOTES

1. Orrin E. Klapp, *Heroes, Villains and Fools: The Changing American Character* (Englewood Cliffs, 1962), pp. 32–33.

Bromden's Spiritual Journey

W.D. Sherman

W.D. Sherman, who taught at University College of
Wales in Aberystwyth, Wales, maintains that Chief
Bromden undergoes the classic process of psychic
death and rebirth prominent in both the psychedelic
and the Buddhist experiences.

Bromden's first step toward death is submitting to the mechanical world of the Combine and relinquishing his own
identity. He acts deaf and dumb precisely because the world
treats him as if he were deaf and dumb, and this loss of self
causes others to view him as a stereotypical "dumb Indian."
His next step in the process is entering a dream state of illusions, evident in the fantastical visions in his "fog." The
dream state also occurs in the hallucinatory phase of a drug
"trip" and is referred to in *The Tibetan Book of the Dead* as
the "Third Bardo of existence." Kesey, according to Sherman,
gains access to Bromden's schizophrenic point of view
through the consciousness-altering drug LSD.

As a psychedelic trip often features a trusted guide, so too
does Bromden's journey feature McMurphy as his guide. In
fighting for the rights of the inmates, McMurphy acts as a
catalyst that forces Bromden to confront his demons, in this
case the Combine, and seek spiritual liberation from them.
Liberation, however, is frightening for Bromden, who has
found safety in remaining invisible. And because willingness
is crucial for a positive drug experience, Bromden's fear and
reluctance sometimes make for a "bad trip."

But he has faith in his guide. In a final, bold act of psychic
liberation, Bromden releases McMurphy's spirit by killing his
physical body—ensuring that the Combine can't make use of
it—and in doing so he releases himself. He frees himself not
only from his guide but from the Combine itself. He is reborn.

Excerpted from W.D. Sherman, "The Novels of Ken Kesey," *Journal of American Studies,* vol. 5, no. 2 (1971), pp. 185–96. Copyright © Cambridge University Press. Reprinted
by permission of Cambridge University Press.

In their manual based upon *The Tibetan Book of the Dead,* Richard Alpert, Ralph Metzner and Timothy Leary discuss the signs of the 'Third Bardo' existence in a psychedelic experience in the vocabulary of Ken Kesey's fiction:

> Where Tibetans saw demons and beasts of prey, a Westerner may see impersonal machinery grinding, or depersonalizing and controlling devices of different futuristic varieties. Visions of world destruction and hallucinations of being engulfed by destructive powers, and sounds of the mind-controlling apparatus of the '*combine's fog machinery*', of the gears which move.[1]

In . . . *One Flew Over The Cuckoo's Nest* . . . Kesey has described that sense of the disintegration and death and ultimate rebirth of the ego which lies at the heart of the LSD 'trip'. [The book is a] literary metaphor for psychedelic experience.

THE CHIEF PLAYS THE GAME

Chief Bromden, the schizoid Indian who narrates the novel, tells the story of Randle Patrick McMurphy, an Irish-American rogue who flies over (and finally 'into') the cuckoo's nest—the madhouse—to avoid work on a prison farm, and who, in the course of the novel, commits himself to the plight of the patients. Bromden is 'mad' only on one level of meaning. What he thinks he is doing is playing the role of a flunky. His existence—as an individual, as an Indian—has been denied by the white world, and so he has played at being deaf and dumb to maintain at least a minimum of freedom.

> I thought it over, about my being deaf, about the years of not letting on I heard what was said, and I wondered if I could ever act any other way again. But I remembered one thing: it wasn't me that started acting deaf; it was people that first started acting like I was too dumb to hear or see anything at all.

Bromden's mind snapped when his father, an Indian chief, tried to accommodate himself to the demands of white men for Indian land. Finally, after Bromden's father married a white woman, he shrivelled up in his son's eyes. 'The Combine. It worked on him for years. He fought it for a long time till my mother made him too little to fight any more and he gave up.' If Bromden is mad, it is because his madness is a result of the strategy he has adopted to live in the hostile

---

1. Richard Alpert, Ralph Metzner, and Timothy Leary, *The Psychedelic Experience* (New York, 1964), p. 80.

white world. In trying to exploit the role which the Combine placed upon him, he plays the dumb Indian, the white man's Indian, the Uncle Tom, for so long that he does, in fact, lose his sanity. His madness is his inability to differentiate the role he has played for so long from 'who he is' as a human being.

QUITTING THE GAME

In the course of the novel, Bromden liberates himself from the clutches of the Combine and declares his freedom from the image which society demands of him. The path he follows is not new, but was first outlined centuries ago in Tibet. He first places himself within the Combine and allows himself to undergo psychic death. Then he enters the dreamstate following psychic death, and, for a time, is caught in this dream-state. He both lives and hides within a world of terrifying illusions; frightened, but temporarily safe in his madness. This is the Third Bardo existence of *The Tibetan Book of the Dead*, which precisely describes a stage in an LSD trip. Kesey describes it this way:

> Right and left there are other things happening just as bad—crazy and horrible things too goofy and outlandish to cry about and too much true to laugh about—but the fog is getting thick enough I don't have to watch. And somebody's tugging at my arm. I know already what will happen: somebody'll drag me out of the fog and we'll be back on the ward and there won't be a sign of what went on tonight and if I was fool enough to try and tell anybody about it they'd say, Idiot, you just had a nightmare; things as crazy as a big machine down in the bowels of a dam where people get cut up by robot workers don't exist. But if they don't exist, how can a man see them?

Bromden descends into the depths of his visions, and this descent 'illustrates the estrangement of consciousness from the liberating truth as it approaches nearer and nearer to physical rebirth', as Jung puts it in his commentary on *The Tibetan Book of the Dead*. Bromden's psychic dissociation, his visions which he believes are produced by a 'fog machine', are the equivalents to the Chonyid State as explained by the Tibetan text. Or, as Jung writes:

> The Chonyid state is equivalent to a deliberately induced psychosis. It is a disintegration of the wholeness of the Bardo body constituting the visible envelope of the psychic self in the after-death state. The psychological equivalent of this dismemberment is dissociation. In its deleterious form it would be schizophre-

nia. . . . The transition to the Chonyid state is a dangerous reversal of the aims and intentions of the conscious mind. It is a sacrifice of the ego's stability and a surrender to the extreme uncertainty of what must seem like a chaotic riot of phantasmal forms. Fear of self-sacrifice lurks deep in every ego, and this fear is often only the precariously controlled demand of the unconscious forces to burst out in full strength. No one who strives for selfhood (individuation) is spared this dangerous passage, for that which is feared also belongs to the wholeness of the self—the sub-human, or supra-human, world of psychic 'dominants' from which the ego originally emancipated itself with enormous effort, and then only partially, for the sake of a more or less illusory freedom. This liberation is certainly a very necessary and very heroic undertaking, but it represents nothing final: it is merely the creation of a subject, who, in order to find fulfillment, has still to be confronted by an object.[2]

LIBERATING THE HUMAN SPIRIT

What I am attempting to point out by restating the parallels between an LSD trip and the states leading to a 'rebirth' described in *The Tibetan Book of the Dead*, and drawing parallels between Bromden's nightmare visions and a bad LSD trip, is this: Kesey is, on the one hand, writing a novel in which his narrator, a mad Indian, tells the story of what happened (and the story of his own 'cure') when Randle Patrick McMurphy decided to do battle against the institutionalized repression of the human spirit; on the other hand, Kesey is suggesting that one path to psychic liberation lies in the psychedelic experience. He does this by paralleling the experiences of his narrator with his own LSD experiences and his knowledge of *The Tibetan Book of the Dead*. Given this context, McMurphy serves a special function: he is Bromden's 'guide'.

McMurphy is the one who induces the 'psychosis' in Bromden, the one who 'turns him on' and forces him to confront the Combine and the 'fog machine'. Bromden, of course, would rather remain 'safe'. He would, on one level of consciousness, rather McMurphy did nothing to aid him on a path to liberation. Bromden has his 'bad trip', his descent into the Third Bardo, precisely *because* McMurphy has forced him to undertake the experience. If a person does not enter into the psychedelic experience willingly, then that person is destined to descend into a psychic hell. The 'set' (predispositions at the beginning of the session), and the

2. Carl Jung, 'Psychological Commentary on *The Tibetan Book of the Dead*', *Psyche & Symbol* (New York, 1958), p. 294.

'setting' (where, when, with whom you have the session), are of key importance. Richard Alpert, writing on who should take LSD, says that the answers to the following questions must all be I 'yes' to ensure a good trip:

1. Can I trust the guide?

2. Could I gain sufficient rapport with him to enter into an explicit verbal contact about the journey?

3. Is the person entering into the session in a fully informed and voluntary fashion?

4. Is this somebody with whom I want to share a psychedelic experience?[3]

LEAVING A 'SAFE' FOG WITH A TRUSTED GUIDE

Obviously, for Kesey's narrator, the answers to these questions are not all in the affirmative. In a paragraph which forms a separate chapter, the shortest chapter in the novel, Bromden says:

> It's getting hard to locate my bed at night, have to crawl around on my hands and knees feeling underneath the springs till I find my gobs of gum stuck there. Nobody complains about all the fog. I know why now: as bad as it is, you can slip back in it and feel safe. That's what McMurphy can't understand, us wanting to be safe. He keeps trying to drag us out of the fog, out in the open where we'd be easy to get at.

As Kesey himself puts it in the dedication of the book to Vik Lovell, the man who first experimented with LSD with the author: 'He told me dragons did not exist/then led me to their lairs.' But it should be kept in mind when reading *One Flew Over The Cuckoo's Nest* that the strength of the novel rests in Kesey's intertwining both levels of the book in such a way that the underlying superstructure—the LSD trip— grows organically, is never superimposed as an 'in-joke'.

Thus when McMurphy, who has been undermining the authority of Big Nurse, who heads the ward, finally realizes that he might have to remain in the hospital for as long a time as she wishes him to be committed, he decides against any further struggle. McMurphy gets 'cagey' as Bromden says; cagey in the way that the Indian's father had. Bromden begins to lose his trust and confidence in McMurphy, and if one loses trust and confidence in one's guide, any trip can only be a series of nightmares.

But McMurphy is not cagey for long. Cheswick, one of the patients, commits suicide because he feels McMurphy has

3. Richard Alpert, *LSD* (New York, 1966), p. 70.

let him down. Stung by Cheswick's death, McMurphy again takes up the struggle. . . .

[He] fights with a Negro aide who is bullying a patient. McMurphy, and the Chief who helped out in the fight, are subjected to electro-shock treatment. Before McMurphy goes under, he whispers 'guts ball' to the Chief, and guts ball is exactly what the Chief plays. Although he too gets the shock treatment, the 'fog machine' in the 'shock shop' fails this time to do its job:

> How many hours have I been out? It's fogging a little, but I won't slip off and hide in it. No, never again. I rubbed my eyes with the heels of my hands and tried to clear my head. I worked at it. I'd never worked at coming out of it before. . . . I saw an aide coming up the hall with a tray for me and knew this time I had them beat. . . .

AN ACT OF INDEPENDENCE: SAYING GOODBYE TO THE GUIDE

McMurphy is lobotomized, and 'it' is pushed into the day room with a tag around its throat. The men look on in disbelief, refusing to accept the fact that what they see in front of them was once a man. They refuse to believe that the Combine has won the final victory. Bromden performs the one necessary remaining act. During the night he smothers what is left of McMurphy, knowing that 'he wouldn't have left something like that sit there in the day room with his name tacked on it for twenty or thirty years so the Big Nurse could use it as an example of what can happen if you buck the system. I was sure of that.'

The Chief's action is not merely the act which will affirm the victory over the Combine (for by killing the body the spirit is released), not even merely the performing of the psychological truism that every man must kill his father. It is a correlative for the act of finally liberating oneself from one's guide on the LSD trip. The realization on the part of the subject of the LSD trip is that one must 'go it alone' and not rely on the previous experience of the guide.

The Chief leaves the mental hospital, and he decides to hitchhike back to his village by the Columbia River near Canada. He wants to see what his tribe has been doing since the government swindled it out of its land. He thinks he might even be able to help. 'I been away a long time', he says as the novel closes.

Big Chief as Narrator and Executioner

Fred Madden

Fred Madden, English professor at Ithaca College, begins his essay by defining two camps of readers: those who view McMurphy as a brave hero and those who view him as a racist and sexist. The two camps seem to have reached a compromise to this enduring controversy, says Madden, by instead focusing on Chief Bromden as the novel's main character. While McMurphy is a vehicle for the Chief, a catalyst who sets his recovery in motion, he is not responsible for the Chief's recovery. The Chief is the one who does the necessary soul-searching in his quest for sanity and freedom. McMurphy, on the other hand, regresses from sanity and freedom by allowing himself to be manipulated by the inmates.

Throughout the novel, the Chief makes great strides in learning to take responsibility for his own actions (rather than avoiding it by retreating into his deaf and dumb "fog"). He learns, one incident at a time, to become independent of McMurphy, and this happens as he becomes increasingly aware of the role his friend is playing. The Chief sees through McMurphy's swaggering bravado to the burdened man he becomes, the target for all the other men's needs. With his new acceptance of responsibility, however, comes guilt—about his own role in the group's slaying of McMurphy, both figuratively and literally. As such, the novel represents the Chief's confession. And although in the end he escapes the hospital, he realizes it is quite a different matter to escape one's own guilt.

One Flew Over the Cuckoo's Nest has elicited continuing critical debate about McMurphy as the novel's hero. Readings fall roughly into two camps: one, because downplaying as-

Excerpted from Fred Madden, "Sanity and Responsibility: Big Chief as Narrator and Executioner," *Modern Fiction Studies*, vol. 32, no. 2 (1986), pp. 203–17. Copyright, Purdue Research Foundation, West Lafayette, Indiana 47907. Edited and reprinted with permission.

pects of McMurphy's racism, sexism, and paternalism, approves of him as a vital, positive figure and the novel's hero; the other, condemning McMurphy, attacks Kesey for glorifying a despicable individual. Those readers who affirm McMurphy's heroism argue that he valiantly confronts the forces of dehumanism and mechanism in our society—forces represented by what Big Chief calls the "combine." But even recent readings that praise McMurphy have the task of either palliating or ignoring what have been seen as McMurphy's racist and sexist biases.[1] Readers condemning McMurphy have pointed both to his language (he calls blacks "coons" four or five times and Washington "a nigger") and to his actions (he seems to take sadistic pleasure in bloodying Washington's nose in a basketball game and in hitting the orderly in the shower room). Other readers have accused McMurphy, and Kesey himself, of sexist attitudes: the "bad" women (Big Nurse, Billy's mother, and Harding's wife) are bitches, and the "good" women are prostitutes with hearts of gold. Readings that emphasize racist and sexist attitudes blame Kesey for creating stereotypical characters who are used to convey a white macho-paternalism that degrades women and blacks.[2]

Emphasis on either McMurphy's positive character traits or his negative ones is largely responsible for the novel's continuing controversy. Readers, lining up on one side or the other, have produced an interpretative stalemate. However, a shift of critical perspective from McMurphy to Big Chief provides a way around this deadlock. For such a reading, Big Chief must be seen as the novel's central character whose narrative records his own movement toward self-reliance and sanity.[3] But, second, this seemingly positive narrative reveals the ward members' and Big Chief's manipulation and destruction of McMurphy. . . .

Big Chief is Kesey's most complex creation in *Cuckoo's Nest* because he is both a character in his own right and one

1. In his *Ken Kesey* Stephen Tanner argues that regardless of his faults, McMurphy must be looked upon as central to the novel's action (18–51). See also Boardman (171–183). There are a number of other readers who find McMurphy the central character. See Baurect, Leeds (13–43), De Bellis "Facing Things Honestly," Beidler, Carnes (5–18), Martin, Sunderland, Barsness. 2. Marcia Y. Falk began the sexist and racist criticism against McMurphy and by implication against Kesey as well. Others to take part in this argument are Forrey, Hort, Bross. For an abridged account of the racist and sexist criticism see Leeds (14–17) and Tanner (44–47). 3. All of the following articles mention the possibility of Big Chief as Kesey's hero: Hardy, Benert, Hunt, Herrenkohl, Sasoon. None emphasizes the importance of the Chief's growth in consciousness as it relates to his self-reliance in the face of group pressure.

A Schizophrenic Point of View

Tom Wolfe is the author of a well-known book about Ken Kesey, entitled The Electric Kool-Aid Acid Test. *In it Kesey recounts his creation of Chief Bromden, the novel's narrator, as the key to* One Flew Over the Cuckoo's Nest.

For some reason peyote does this . . . Kesey starts getting eyelid movies of faces, whole galleries of weird faces, churning up behind the eyelids, faces from out of nowhere. He knows nothing about Indians and has never met an Indian, but suddenly here is a full-blown Indian—Chief Broom—the solution, the whole mothering key, to the novel. . . .

From the point of view of craft, Chief Broom was his great inspiration. If he had told the story through McMurphy's eyes, he would have had to end up with the big bruiser delivering a lot of homilies about his down-home theory of mental therapy. Instead, he told the story through the Indian. This way he could present a schizophrenic state the way the schizophrenic himself, Chief Broom, feels it and at the same time report the McMurphy Method more subtly.

Tom Wolfe, *The Electric Kool-Aid Acid Test.* New York: Farrar, Straus and Giroux, 1968, pp. 42–44.

whose perspective controls the reader's. Although the Chief cannot be termed a character who intentionally attempts to deceive, he is a character whose insanity *and humanity* cause him to distort facts in ways that disclose Kesey's preoccupation with people's dehumanization of themselves and others.

Big Chief's distorted perspective reveals truths about the extent of dehumanization on the ward because much of his bizarre behavior is an attempt to avoid this dehumanization. His "deaf and dumb act" offers him a way out of degrading situations, but the problem with this tactic becomes evident to Big Chief when he finds the alienation of the "fog" more frightening than the hostile environment of Big Nurse's ward. In avoiding the outside world and retreating into the "fog," the Chief comes up against the terrifying sense of being alone without identity.

As Big Chief moves toward sanity, he begins to break out of the bind of having to choose either the hostile world or his own alienation. McMurphy, as a catalyst, may be partially responsible for prodding the Chief toward recovery, but Kesey wants the reader to see that Big Chief's sanity results from his own actions, especially after his last electroshock treatment when the Chief knows he "had them beat."

There is, however, for the Chief no quick avenue to sanity, which seems to come mainly from his increasing sense of responsibility for his own actions. His first significant act is his vote in favor of the World Series. Initially the Chief attempts to believe that McMurphy is making him raise his hand by means of "wires." But immediately after making this assertion the Chief takes responsibility and says that he "lifted it" himself. This first acceptance of responsibility leads to others: his decision to go on the fishing trip, his support of McMurphy in fighting the orderlies, and his quick recovery from his last shock treatment.

McMurphy Responsible for Chief's Recovery?

What often happens, however, is an attempt by readers to give McMurphy exclusive credit for the Chief's growing sanity. Yet Big Chief is the only one of the ward members who gains his sanity. If McMurphy acts as a catalyst to sanity, all of the other Acutes presumably should have benefited as well. Only the Chief, however, is meant to be seen as sane at the end.

Read carefully, the novel reveals the pattern of Big Chief's slowly growing sanity independent of McMurphy's aid. Twenty pages after he has voted in favor of the World Series, the Chief gets out of bed alone to look at the autumn night. Here he begins to recapture some of his former feelings about nature as he watches a dog wander about in the moonlight. That the dog is run over by a car reinforces the images of the power of the machine over the organic world, but the event doesn't distress Big Chief. In fact, the extensively birthmarked nurse who puts the Chief to bed might seem less sane than he does. This whole incident is independent of McMurphy's presence and points to Big Chief's growing individualism.

Immediately after the above incident, McMurphy begins to "get cagey" because he learns that Big Nurse has control over his length of commitment. In relationship to the pattern of the novel Kesey is suggesting that Big Chief is increasingly able to strengthen his self-reliance while McMurphy loses his: specifically, when McMurphy capitulates to the pressure of the ward members and becomes their leader once again at the end of this section.

In the next section, when McMurphy becomes the ward's leader once again, the Chief begins to remember his childhood in detail, independent of McMurphy's, or anyone else's, influence. Because these rather lengthy memories precede McMurphy's offer of gum, it seems likely that they can be seen to have some influence on Big Chief's decision to speak. Take for instance a passage that occurs seven pages before the Chief speaks: "I lay in bed all night . . . and thought it over, about my being deaf, about the years of not letting on I heard what was said and I wondered if I could ever act any other way again." The memory that follows this quotation bears directly on the reasons why Big Chief began his "deaf and dumb" act; it is his memory of when he was treated as "invisible" by the federal agents who wanted the Chief's tribal land. After the memory, he is already predisposed to begin talking when he finds Geever taking the gum from under his bed. Such an argument does not deny McMurphy as a catalyst agent, but rather it emphasizes Big Chief's active part in preparing himself for sanity.

Speaking After EST

Big Chief's active role is most clear when he has his last electroshock treatment, after which he is able to speak to others and no longer feigns deafness—a change meant to indicate his growing sanity and ability to cope. Surprisingly little attention has been given Big Chief's fragmented thoughts immediately before his recovery from his last electroshock treatment. If, however, these thoughts are seen in the context of Big Chief's attempt to find a viable individualistic option for his life, the section makes sense. As the Chief searches his memory, images of dice coming up "snake eyes" indicate his rejection of possible options:

> My roll. *Faw.* Damn. Twisted again. Snake eyes.
>
> The schoolteacher tell me you got a good head, boy, be something. . . .
>
> Be what, Papa? A rug-weaver like Uncle R & J Wolf? A blanket-weaver? or another drunken Indian?
>
> I say, attendant, you're an Indian, aren't you?
>
> Yeah, that's right.
>
> Well, I must say, you speak the language quite well.
>
> Yeah.
>
> Well . . . three dollars of regular.
>
> They wouldn't be so cocky if they knew what me and the *moon* have going. No damned regular indian . . .
>
> He who—what is it?—walks out of step, hears another drum.
>
> Snake eyes again. Hoo boy, these dice are *cold.*

In this passage Big Chief rejects the standard options, from rug-weaver to alcoholic, available to an Indian in white or Indian society. At the end of the passage he also rejects his possible role as rebel (intimated by the paraphrasing of Thoreau's words). Ultimately Big Chief does not want to be cast in the role either of conformist or of rebel because both end with "snake eyes."

If Big Chief rejects both conformity and rebellion, what option is left for him? Here the dice imagery is important because at the end of the section the Chief sees that he has been loading the dice against himself. Only after this realization can he "work himself out of" the shock treatment. When he takes responsibility for his own actions, he knows he has "them beat."

Seeing McMurphy in a New Light

After his recovery from this, his last shock treatment, the Chief is able to see McMurphy from a less idealized perspective. He becomes aware that McMurphy forces himself to continue to take shock treatments because "every one of those faces on Disturbed had turned toward him and was waiting." Although McMurphy attempts to pose as a heroic figure who can take anything that Big Nurse "dishes out," Big Chief sees through the role: "But every time that loud speaker called for him to forgo breakfast and prepare to walk to Building One, the muscles in his jaw went taut and his whole face drained of color, *looking thin and scared*—the fact I had seen reflected in the windshield on the trip back from the coast" (italics mine). Group pressure forces McMurphy to play the role of hero, but the result is the draining of his individuality.

When Big Chief returns from his last electroshock treatment, he begins to understand the power exerted on him by the ward members. They begin to look at him as a hero: "everybody's face turned up to me with a different look than they'd ever given me before." And, as a result, Big Chief begins to realize "how McMurphy must've felt all these months with these faces screaming up at him." The ward members are ready to see the former "deaf and dumb Injun" as a glorious "Wildman," but Kesey's point is that neither of these roles reflects the Chief's real self. "Injun" and "Wildman" are roles that the group defines or has defined.

Group Dynamics in the Ward

Perhaps Big Chief is the only character who actually maintains an awareness of his personal involvement in the process of playing roles at the end of the novel. To a large extent this awareness is the result of watching McMurphy become trapped by his roles. It is not by chance, then, that Big Chief kills McMurphy. It is not a mercy killing as some readers have argued, or an act of love, or a murder of the Chief's former self.[4] The murder is best understood in light of both group pressure and individual realization. It is the Chief's last action as part of the group, and through it Big Chief is able to understand fully the extent to which McMurphy and he have been manipulated by the ward members. This awareness of the power of groups allows him to free himself from the members and to define himself as an individual.

As one of the ward's members, Big Chief acts in the manner of a priest/executioner of a primitive society. The title of the novel is derived from a nursery rhyme, and . . . counting rhymes were often used by "primitive tribes" to "select the human sacrifice offered to appease a wrathful god." The idea of a sacrifice is apropos: not in order to "appease a wrathful god" but rather as the result of the ward members' need to manipulate and destroy a victim both as a demonstration of their own power and as a way to scapegoat the guilt resulting from the destruction of the individual.

The notion that Kesey intended McMurphy as a sacrificial victim finds support in the novel. When McMurphy returns from the lobotomy, Big Chief denies that the lobotomized form has a name—a denial comparable to a ritual common to sacrifices: the victim's namelessness before sacrifice. Big Chief, however, attempts to argue that McMurphy's form will be used by Big Nurse as an example to others of what happens to those who buck the system. In reality, the ward members themselves are more responsible for McMurphy's destruction than Big Nurse is.

THE CHIEF KILLS "IT"

Big Chief, however, is more than simply an executioner performing the will of the ward members who have sacrificed McMurphy's individualism to their own manipulative needs. Earlier in the novel, Big Chief had seen McMurphy as "a giant come out of the sky to save us from the 'Combine.'" Later he

---

4. The most recent of the novel's readers to see McMurphy's death as a result of mercy killing is Leeds (42). Those seeing the murder as an act of love are Gallagher, Baurect (291), Beidler (58), Sherwood (108). Those who view McMurphy's death as Big Chief's murder of his former self are De Bellis ("Alone No More" 73) and Waldmeir (202).

sacrifices "this giant" not to the "Combine" but to fulfill the collective will of the ward members, which is inseparably his own. It is immediately after he kills McMurphy that Big Chief realizes the extent of his own manipulation and his responsibility in McMurphy's death.

It is interesting that Big Chief deflects this realization from direct expression:

> I lay for a while, holding the covers over my face, and thought I was being pretty quiet, but Scanlon's voice hissing from his bed let me know I wasn't.
>
> "Take it easy, Chief," he said. "Take it easy. It's okay."

Big Chief's crying here might be explained as the result of his grief over having to destroy the lobotomized form of his onetime friend and leader, McMurphy. But more is suggested if Big Chief's reaction is connected with his description of the actual murder:

> The big, hard body had a tough grip on life. It fought a long time against having it taken away, flailing and thrashing around so much I finally had to lie full length on top of it and scissor the kicking legs with mine while I mashed the pillow into the face. I lay there on top of the body for what seemed days. Until the thrashing stopped. Until it was still a while and had shuddered once and was still again.

What is noticeable about this description is its dehumanization of McMurphy, who is referred to as "it" or "the body." Here Big Chief, fulfilling his role as the ward member's priest/executioner, has completely dehumanized another human being. Viewed in the context of Big Chief's murder of McMurphy, it might seem ironic that so much attention has been paid to McMurphy's sexist and racist postures in the novel. They may be indefensible, but in the novel their expression as an indication of an individual's prejudice and stereotyping might be judged as less menacing and destructive than the type of dehumanization that is socially enforced.

In killing McMurphy, Big Chief has, as the ward's "representative," direct experience of the power of a social group over an individual. He has been both a participant in exerting the group's power and a witness in recording the effect of that power on the individual. He cries after McMurphy's death because he realizes that both he and McMurphy not only have been used by the ward members but also have accepted the roles that the members have provided for them—executioner and victim. In rejecting McMurphy's cap as too small, Big

Chief also rejects his attachment to any social role because it can lead only to the roles of victimizer or victim. In his rejection of the social role that led to McMurphy's lobotomy and murder, Big Chief proves that he is "bigger" than any of the other characters. He is able to understand the terrible power of groups and, more than that, the power of the individual to reject social control. It is this second realization that leads to his escape from the institution and his freedom.

ESCAPE TO NOWHERE?

Such an escape, as uplifting as it might appear in relationship to the assertion of an individual's freedom, is not without qualification in the novel. A question might be raised about what exactly Big Chief escapes to. There is some suggestion that he might become like the other Indians who "are spearing salmon in the spillway" below the "big hydroelectric dam," an image of the survival of individualism under the immensity of the technocratic superstructure of American society. However, his main preference is "to look over the country around the gorge again" because, as he says, "I been away a long time."

On the surface, this rather tentative ending, bordering on nostalgia, does not seem a potent enough answer to the socially destructive forces that Big Chief escapes. But the Chief's last line, "I been away a long time," also echoes Huck Finn's last line, "I been there before" (Clemens 299).[5] And likewise, Big Chief's escape to The Dalles may be reminiscent of the impossibility of Huck's complete escape from social forces by being "ahead of the rest." But the connection between Huck Finn and Big Chief is not simply one of tentative escapes. Both are storytellers who recount their pasts and, in so doing, reveal their inability to escape. In each novel the reader is given little about the possibilities of each of these characters' lives after their respective escapes to freedom. The only definite action is the narration of the story itself. However, there is a paradox in the telling of each story because in doing so the narrator still is tied to the social forces he has supposedly escaped. On one level, the narration recounts an individual's escape. Simultaneously, on another level, the narration reveals

5. I would like to thank Kevin Murphy for pointing out the similarity between Huck's and Big Chief's last lines and for suggesting numerous improvements and emendations in my manuscript. See also his first-rate article on the effects of literacy on Huck Finn.

an individual's inability fully to escape because the individual independence that is formed in repudiation of society is also inextricably linked to it.

FREEDOM AND GUILT

In *Cuckoo's Nest* the Chief's growth in his sense of responsibility for his own actions leads ultimately to his escape from the asylum. But that same responsibility carries with it the burden of guilt for his role in murdering McMurphy. The individual responsibility that allows Big Chief to escape also binds him to his past actions in the asylum. When Big Chief played deaf and dumb at the beginning of *Cuckoo's Nest*, he may have swung from his alienation in the "fog" to his fear of the hostile world of the ward, but he did not feel any guilt. Guilt, however, drives Big Chief's narration, which must finally be seen as confessional: "It's gonna burn me just that way, finally telling about all this, about the hospital, and her, and the guys—and about McMurphy. I been silent so long now it's gonna roar out of me like floodwaters. . . ." The "truth even if it really didn't happen" is the Chief's final inability to escape the ward because his shadowy sense of freedom at the end is irrevocably tied to his escape from the asylum. The act of murder that allows the Chief to realize his own and McMurphy's manipulation at the hands of the ward members is the same act that, because of his newly acquired sense of responsibility, produces the guilt that drives the narration. By the end of the novel Big Chief has traded his initial freedom from guilt (due to his personal denial of responsibility for his own actions) for a freedom from social control (due to his acceptance of responsibility and its attendant guilt). It is perhaps fitting then that Big Chief's narration should begin as if he were once again back on the ward.

WORKS CITED

Barsness, John A. "Ken Kesey: The Hero in Modern Dress." *Bulletin of the Rocky Mountain Modern Language Association* 23 (1969): 27–33.

Baurect, William C. "Separation, Initiation, and Return: Schizophrenic Episode in *One Flew Over the Cuckoo's Nest*." *Midwest Quarterly* 23 (1982): 279–293.

Beidler, Peter G. "From Rabbits to Men: Self-Reliance in the Cuckoo's Nest." *Lex et Scientia* 13 (1977): 56–59.

Benert, Annette. "The Forces of Fear: Kesey's Anatomy of Insanity." *Lex et Scientia* 13 (1977): 22–26.

Boardman, Michael M. *"One Flew Over the Cuckoo's Nest:* Rhetoric and Vision." *Journal of Narrative Technique* 9 (1979): 171–183.

Bross, Addison C. "Art and Ideology: Kesey's Approach to Fiction." *Lex et Scientia* 13 (1977): 60–64.

Carnes, Bruce. *Ken Kesey.* Boise State University Western Writers Series 12. Boise: Boise State UP, 1974.

Clemens, Samuel L. *Adventures of Huckleberry Finn.* 1885. New York: Norton, 1977.

De Bellis, Jack. "Alone No More: Dualism in American Literary Thought." *Lex et Scientia* 13 (1977): 73.

———. "Facing Things Honestly: McMurphy's Conversion." *Lex et Scientia* 13 (1977): 11–13.

Falk, Marcia Y. Letter. *New York Times* 5 Dec. 1971. Rpt. in *"One Flew Over the Cuckoo's Nest": Text and Criticism.* Ed. John C. Pratt. New York: Viking, 1973. 450–453.

Forrey, Robert. "Ken Kesey's Psychopathic Savior: A Rejoinder." *Modern Fiction Studies* 21 (1975): 222–230.

Gallagher, Edward J. "From Folded Hands to Clenched Fists: Kesey and Science Fiction." *Lex et Scientia* 13 (1977): 49–50.

Grunwald, Beverly. "Kesey: A Sane View from *Cuckoo's Nest." Women's Wear Daily* Dec. 1975: 1–3.

Hardy, William J. "Chief Bromden: Kesey's Existentialist Hero." *North Dakota Quarterly* 18 (1980): 72–83.

Herrenkohl, Ellen. "Regaining Freedom: Sanity in Insane Places." *Lex et Scientia* 13 (1977): 42–44.

Hort, Leslie. "Bitches, Twitches, and Eunuchs: Sex Role Failure and Caricature." *Lex et Scientia* 13 (1977): 14–17.

Hunt, John W. "Flying the Cuckoo's Nest: Kesey's Narrator as Norm." *Lex et Scientia* 13 (1977): 26–32.

Kesey, Ken. *Kesey's Garage Sale.* New York: Viking, 1973.

———. *One Flew Over the Cuckoo's Nest.* New York: Viking, 1962.

Leeds, Barry H. *Ken Kesey.* New York: Ungar, 1981.

Lish, Gordon. "'What the Hell You Looking in Here For, Daisy Mae?' An Interview with Ken Kesey." *Genesis West* 2 (1963): 17–29.

Martin, Terence. "*One Flew Over the Cuckoo's Nest* and the High Cost of Living." *Modern Fiction Studies* 19 (1973): 43–55.

Murphy, Kevin. "Illiterate's Progress: The Descent into Literacy in *Huckleberry Finn*." *Texas Studies in Literature and Language* 26 (1984): 363–387.

Sasoon, R.L. Rev. of *One Flew Over the Cuckoo's Nest. Northwest Review* 6 (1963): 116–120.

Sherwood, Terry G. "*One Flew Over the Cuckoo's Nest* and the Comic Strip." *Critique*, 13 (1971): 96–109.

Sunderland, Janet R. "A Defense of Ken Kesey's *One Flew Over the Cuckoo's Nest.*" *English Journal* 61 (1972): 28–31.

Tanner, Stephen L. *Ken Kesey.* Twayne's United States Authors Series 444. Boston: Twayne, 1983.

Waldmeir, Joseph J. "Two Novelists of the Absurd: Heller and Kesey." *Wisconsin Studies in Contemporary Literature* 5 (1964): 192–204.

CHAPTER 4

Cuckoo's Nest on Film

The Film Compared to the Novel

Frank Kermode

Books rarely make good movies, according to Frank Kermode, eminent modernist literary critic and author of many books. *One Flew Over the Cuckoo's Nest* film director Milos Forman compensates by basing his movie version loosely, or "crudely," as Kermode says, on the original. Obvious similarities are the characters and basic plot. Differences include the addition of comic elements to the movie and, most importantly, the point of view.

Favoring an "objective narration," Forman has scrapped the use of the schizophrenic Chief Bromden as the story's narrator. We do not see things, as we did in the novel, through the hallucinated vision of a disturbed mental patient. Thus the texture of the movie is significantly different from that of the book. Foreman instead moves the story along through the artistically photographed faces of the remarkable actors Louise Fletcher (Nurse Ratched) and Jack Nicholson (McMurphy). Their performances, says Kermode, capture the "modern . . . yet mythological conflicts" portrayed in *Cuckoo's Nest*. Keeping things simple, Foreman lets their "wonderfully expressive set of faces" tell the story.

Films based on good, or even quite good, books usually make little more than unmemorable thin allusions to their originals; some version of the fable is certainly preserved, but the subject or discourse tends to be dissipated by the camera and the soundtrack. Novels are arguably the least suitable "material" for movies. . . .

[Director] Milos Forman seems conscious of the difficulty and seeks, with some success, to overcome it by implanting

Excerpted from Frank Kermode, "Men, Women, and Madness," *The London Times Literary Supplement*, March 19, 1976. Reprinted by permission of the author.

in his film of *One Flew Over the Cuckoo's Nest* a strongly drawn diagram—coarsely drawn, I was going to say—of Ken Kesey's theme, and so buying himself the right to provide the film with a texture resembling very little in the original, though in itself more than adequately interesting. The effect is curious: the audience is moved to cry out with approval and sympathy as the hero struggles to outwit his oppressors: a very simple reaction indeed, yet produced while the screen is filled with the subtle and delicate visual images made by Haskell Wexler's camera. Here, perhaps, is the beginning of an explanation of the mixed feelings the film produces, embarrassment and pleasure among them. . . .

Milos Forman offers a few cautiously expressed remarks about what he had been trying to do. The narrator in the novel is a schizophrenic Indian; Forman altered this, not simply because of the obvious difficulties but because he prefers "objective narration". Nurse Ratched, the principal tormentor of the inmates of the hospital, is to be represented, not as she is in the Chief's disturbed mind—manipulator of a vast array of coercive electronic and mechanical devices—but as something much more characteristic of the times, a person who does harm by strict loyalty to a perverse belief. . . .

FEAR OF FAITH—PRAISE FROM PRIESTS

Milos Forman admits that he knows little about mental illness, adding that he didn't need to. Life in the madhouse is a figure for life in society; most of the victims are undergoing their brainwashing voluntarily; only people in authority are full of passionate intensity. Forman fears faith, the force that animates Nurse Ratched. As an atheist he was, he says, surprised when a group of priests who saw the film in Washington congratulated him on having made so religious a movie, and explained its symbolism in detail. When the Indian wrenches out the heavy shower control unit and throws it through the window he is rolling back the stone before the tomb, and his escape is a figure for the Resurrection. But another reason for his feeling that this was a peculiar reaction to his work is that he believes the *lieu privilégié* [privileged place] of drama is the human face; and it is true that he attends to faces very lovingly, and at the expense of the symbol-forming potential of all the clutter he could have put in instead.

The film is almost as simple as he claims. There is the face of Ratched, ball-breaker, emblem of society and Mom;

and the face of doomed, rebellious, male McMurphy, and the Indian's beautiful face; and the variously oppressed faces of the other inmates. On these faces the whole play is played out. Yet the priests were right in detecting the presence of symbolism; it arises inevitably from a certain crudeness in the thematic diagram as the film exposes it.

SIMILARITIES AND DIFFERENCES BETWEEN NOVEL AND FILM

Ken Kesey's novel had a small cult in the early 1960s. Then, for a while, the times seemed to be strongly on its side. The Nurse easily merged into fashionable concepts such as Repressive Tolerance, her patients into its compliant victims, endorsing her worst tyrannies by democratic vote, even when she denies them the primordial right of American males to watch the World Series on television, and mental hospitals became images not of hell but of the Larger Society. . . .

[McMurphy] watches Ratched unman the other inmates, resists almost successfully, and is finally lobotomized-castrated. But before that he has helped to arrange the sexual initiation of Billy, a mother-ruined youth (an episode greatly developed in the film), and has formed a love-alliance with the sham-catatonic Indian (also altered and developed). Billy rises from the bed of a life-enhancing whore liberated, freed of his stammer; only to be reduced again to impotence, and eventually to suicide, by Ratched's reassertion of the perpetual maternal threat. McMurphy himself is lovingly murdered by the Indian in a scene of quasi-sexual violence. The Indian alone escapes.

Milos Forman's claim to have been faithful to the book has to be qualified in obvious ways. Some additions are for laughs: for example, the wild party with the whores and the basketball game dominated by the huge Indian. This is founded on a mere hint in the novel, and is there for the sake of showing the big man rising comically from defeat, dropping the ball into the absurdly low basket and lumbering expressionlessly about the court. Very broad, but perhaps the least offensive of the bedlamizing scenes in the film; for we do sometimes feel we are at that kind of exhibition. Other justified amendments are pure film and impossible in novels, like the interview between McMurphy and the doctor, half-ruined himself by Ratched, uneasily complicit in the patient's unreconstructed maleness; a wonderfully acted moment.

What is most obviously missing is precisely that ambiguity as to facts and attitudes that Ken Kesey got by means of his schizoid narrator. The effect is that the film seems simpler, more mythological than the novel. And for this change in the sense of the story I think we must blame or thank critic Leslie Fiedler. He admired the book from the start, and thanks to him it is impossible to think of it without thinking of that long line of American fictions about the flight of the male from female sexuality. McMurphy is an adult Huck [Finn]. The hilarious fishing trip (also much enlarged in the movie) on which McMurphy takes the inmates is Huck hanging up a sign saying "Gone fishin'". The Chief is his Jim ("our greatest Negro characters, including Nigger Jim, are, at their most moving moments, red men in black face"), or the aboriginal love of a new Natty Bumppo [hero of Cooper's *Leatherstocking Tales*]; and it is the aborigine who lopes off at the end, having freed himself from paleface treachery, into the blue Oregon hills. Leslie Fiedler wanted to incorporate the book into a more modern myth also, making the Indian a guru; his madness, he tells us, was modelled on Ken Kesey's experience with LSD. But what stuck was the more primitive version; and it is this version that Milos Forman's film reinforces. . . .

It is in the faces of Forman's actors that we observe the conflict. They are more than adequate to the task. Louise Fletcher as the Nurse has devised a limited but wonderfully expressive set of faces: a smile of nightmare rightness and kindness which shifts, with little perceptible alteration, into a mask of hatred and menace that is still somehow *right*, forbearing. Jack Nicholson's performance is at least as remarkable; cunning, attractive, antinomian, life-enhancing, destructive, coming only slowly to an understanding of the deadly nature of the game he is in; and we are dragged into exactly the measure of complicity shown by the doctor in the scene I mentioned. These are dream faces, actualized with extraordinary intelligence. And if nothing else in novel or film were worth taking seriously these faces are: wholly modern, yet the *lieux privilégiés* of dark mythological conflicts.

An Adolescent Fantasy

David Denby

Director Milos Forman's *One Flew Over the Cuckoo's Nest* is little more than an attempt to be "a hip entertainment for kids," claims David Denby, a prominent writer on cultural matters whose most recent book is *Great Books* (1996). It gives its audience a chance to vicariously relive such youthful naughtiness as "tricking the teacher." But for young and old audiences alike, the film's message is not so innocent; rather, says Denby, "it doesn't always say the benign things it thinks it is saying."

One of the film's main offenses is its blatant misogyny, or women-hating. The depiction of the lead female character as an utterly evil monster fosters hatred—evident when the audience cheers when she is physically assaulted. (This despite a "marvelous" performance by Louise Fletcher as Nurse Ratched.) Jack Nicholson as an egotistical, self-righteous McMurphy—the beloved "role model" for whom the audience cheers—seems like a child having a temper tantrum, his assault on the Nurse more than a little sexually perverse. Another offense, according to Denby, is Forman's stabs at comedy at the expense of the mentally disabled; one must stop and ask whether it is in good taste to create caricatures of the insane, to turn "freaks into good theater."

Denby cites the film's total unbelievability as the ultimate flaw. "How many nurses have this kind of power?" he asks. Not to be taken seriously, *One Flew Over the Cuckoo's Nest* is a product of Kesey's and Forman's imaginations—it is fantastical, a fantasy, by its very nature not credible.

Most people do their best to bury their emotions of late adolescence as they get older, so a movie that bring us back to the way we felt at 16 is a force to be reckoned with. If the

Reprinted from David Denby, "*Cuckoo's Nest* Is Just an Adolescent Fantasy," *The New York Times*, December 21, 1975, section 2, page 17, by permission of the author.

movie also appeals to actual 16-year-olds, it's bound to be a hit.

Milos Forman's adaptation of Ken Kesey's novel "One Flew Over the Cuckoo's Nest" evokes powerful feelings of victimization and rebellion. Jack Nicholson's free-living redneck, imprisoned in a state mental hospital for "observation," leads a doomed revolt of the patients against a tyrannical nurse whose weapons include electro-shock treatment and lobotomy. The theater comes alive with communal memories of playing tricks on the teacher and horsing around after lights out, the awesome mysteries of conspiratorial friendship, loyalty, and hero worship. Yet there are elements in the movie's appeal that are rather squalid; it doesn't always say the benign things it thinks it is saying.

Written in 1960 and 1961, "Cuckoo's Nest," which became a prime text of the 60's counterculture, was imbued with the Freudian clichés and the anti-conformist bitterness of the late fifties. Kesey's great antagonists now seem like stock characters: on the one side, Nurse Ratched, destroying any signs of spirit in her male patients; on the other, Randle Patrick McMurphy, a proletarian version of the Rainmaker–Mr. Roberts redeemer figure who appeared in numerous fifties plays and movies.

Since the hospital and the nurse are largely unbelievable (how many nurses have this kind of power?), the book has been read by many as a parable of America's seemingly gentle but ultimately deadly suppression of its dissident spirits. However, Kesey sexualizes the struggle in ways that are peculiar and self-serving, compromising any such "political" or "social" interpretation. He is perhaps the first writer in over 200 years to see insanity in men as a form of moral weakness (an attitude preserved in the movie), specifically a failure of masculine nerve. His surrogate McMurphy, using wildness and revolt as therapy, helps the frightened men defeat the woman in their lives and, by implication, defeat the "woman" in themselves. McMurphy is literally the bringer of heterosexual potency (Kesey's thunderbolt imagery suggests a hipster-Zeus descended from the Oregon forests), just as Ratched is literally the destroyer of potency.

Of course Kesey's revolt was only for men: his women are either "good chicks," willing to sleep with anyone the hero asks them to, or power-mad, castrating monsters. (It's strange that a book so hostile to conventional therapy should depend so heavily on Freudian ideas for its characterization.) A political book? More than anything else, "Cuckoo's Nest" expresses the fear of being under a woman's power, particularly a mother's power; perhaps only in America, with our tradition of macho-paranoid literature, could such a restricted, bizarrely misogynist fantasy be taken seriously as a statement about freedom and repression.

Screenwriters Lawrence Hauben and Bo Goldman have remained faithful to the novel's misogyny and to its hero-worshipping tone; and by discarding Kesey's first-person narration they've dramatized the Ratched-McMurphy struggle even more directly. Yet despite Louise Fletcher's marvelous performance, the struggle remains fraudulent. Miss Fletcher gives us a genteel monster, a woman dangerously blind to her own anger and love of power, squelching her patients' manhood with the blandest of smiles. We understand the kind of vicious rectitude the actress is striving for, but the role *as written* still lacks the credibility and ordinary human complication that would allow it to escape the grips of Kesey's fantasy.

Watching Nicholson lead a revolt of the sons against this corrupt Big Mama, I looked for a touch of irony; but although Nicholson is often funny in a scabrous way, he seems earnestly to believe that he's involved in a deadly struggle for freedom and human dignity. There's a touch of self-righteousness in his glowering hostility, and more than a touch of sacrificial piety—as if to say, "None of you is worth saving, but I'll do it out of *noblesse oblige.*"

Milos Forman's direction is really good only in those quiet moments when the patients' infantile games and vague hostilities make us feel the pathos of time passing by. Like Kesey, the Czech director does not seem terribly sympathetic to the patients, and his lack of compassion probably helps at the box office. His penchant for grotesque comedy and for rubbing our noses in the sordid "reality" of nuthouse life seems designed to make the film a hip entertainment for kids. However, I don't think Forman's commercial acumen should be taken for some sort of dark comic insight. A paraplegic hacks at a punching bag from his wheelchair; wine is squirted into a catatonic's mouth and it dribbles onto his face and chest—are these really examples of Forman's celebrated "middle-European comic sensibility" that some people have been praising (with knowing references to Kafka), or just examples of stupid bad taste?

I have seen a number of serious films set in mental institutions, harrowing documentaries in which the filmmakers did not exploit the material. But I find something offensive in Forman's turning freaks into "good theater." When Peter Brook did this in his stage and movie productions of Peter Weiss's "Marat/Sade," the stylization and distancing devices alerted us to the didactic nature of the material, but in "Cuckoo's Nest" Forman has played for melodrama and "realism" and audience involvement, and people who are naive about acting and directing techniques are not likely to realize how thoroughly they've been manipulated. Isn't it a bit embarrassing that this supposed paean to freedom and spontaneity is so coercively structured that when Nicholson finally jumps on Louise Fletcher and tries to strangle her to death, many people in the audience break into applause? I'm not sure that that's the kind of audience reaction a director should be proud of. Maybe it would be better if some of those buried adolescent feelings were allowed to rest after all.

Nicholson's Ironic Portrayal of McMurphy

Molly Haskell

Molly Haskell wrote *From Reverence to Rape: The Treatment of Women in the Movies* in 1974 and followed up with *Holding My Own in No Man's Land* in 1997. Here she calls Jack Nicholson's performance as Randle Patrick McMurphy nothing short of "miraculous." Unlike the larger-than-life character in the novel, Nicholson's McMurphy is softened and more human. Haskell notes the difference in acting styles between Nicholson and actor Kirk Douglas, who was originally cast to play the part.

Similarly, writes Haskell, actress Louise Fletcher has turned Nurse Ratched into a more sympathetic human character (though still dangerous), with real flaws and a softness underlying her hard exterior. Rather than representing an entire evil institution, she is characterized in the film as a person who is herself disturbed, one who has experienced "an earlier trauma [and] an arrested emotional development." This is in keeping with director Milos Forman's other efforts to distance his film from the hallucinatory '60s quality of the book, creating instead a movie with "a buoyant feeling of a comic ballet." His rejection of Chief Bromden as narrator is one such effort, not only because a subjective point of view is more appropriate for books than for films, but because it is too artificial and reminiscent of a "trippy" stream-of-consciousness drug experience.

Haskell quotes director Forman defending his use of real mental patients as both subjects and actors (the film was shot on location at the Oregon State Hospital). He sees this as realistic and even therapeutic. One patient, he says, began to speak after years of silence and left the hospital shortly after the film was made, just like Chief Bromden. "Why shouldn't insane people seem more appealing?" Forman asks.

Excerpted from Molly Haskell, "Nicholson Kneads a Fine Madness," *The Village Voice*, December 1, 1975, pp. 126–27. Reprinted by permission of the author.

Dare I admit it: It wasn't until after I had seen Milos Forman's movie of "One Flew Over the Cuckoo's Nest" that I finally read Ken Kesey's 1962 novel all the way through. And having read it, I must say I'm not sorry to have Jack Nicholson's features imprinted upon, and modifying forever in my mind, the image of R.P. McMurphy. . . .

NEITHER "WOMAN'S MAN" NOR "MAN'S MAN"

The mere presence of Nicholson in the role of McMurphy, and Louise Fletcher . . . as Nurse Ratched, are an indication of the degree to which Forman has softened Kesey's archetypes into life-sized characters. Fletcher's Nurse Ratched, squinty-eyed but handsome, a small voice belying a steel will, is younger than her literary prototype, and more realistically disturbing. With her '40s hairstyle and her frozen femininity there is a hint (and Forman, in an interview-conversation we had in his hotel room after the film, confirmed this as deliberate) of an earlier trauma, an arrested emotional development. (I am not sure that even this is adequate. Ironically, in making her three-dimensional, Forman has made us want to know, and understand, more.) As for Nicholson, he is nothing short of miraculous in the role of McMurphy.

In the stage play, a thoroughly conventional, "Mr. Roberts"-against-the-institution type of comedy (which was, I believe, repudiated by Kesey), the role was taken by Kirk Douglas. And it was Douglas actually who acquired the movie rights and originally sought Forman to direct. But due to some missed connections on the closely-watched Czech frontier, the two never made contact, and by the time Forman was brought in on the project Douglas felt he was too old to play the part, and Nicholson had been signed on. Even though Nicholson preceded Forman as a condition of the film, he seems to sum up Forman's angle of vision and modified approach to the material.

The difference between Douglas's strutting, chin-jutting, smile-curling bravura and Nicholson's less physical, self-mocking style is the difference between a rooster and a bantam, between straight and ironic braggadocio. Nicholson is no "woman's man"; he can take them or leave them, which has made him less than a favorite with many women viewers I know. But he is not quite a man's man either. There is too much ironic self-awareness, too much distance and doubt between him and the jock ritual of male cama-raderie. . . .

FROM BOOK TO MOVIE

Forman has eliminated the cruder details, and softened the boisterous, hallucinatory quality of Kesey's "trip" into a choreographed fantasy, with the lunatics, the disenfran-chised, banding together for a few brief moments of shared joy. Occasionally, Forman's projection of a . . . romantic lyri-cism onto adult men seems *too* soft. There are moments of Hollywood sentimentality when these "holy fools" coalesce with an esprit de corps that would seem unlikely in a far more "adjusted" or homogeneous group. But as individuals, they are remarkable: William Redfield as Harding, the "in-tellectual" of the group, Brad Dourif as the heartbreakingly

AN OSCAR-WINNING PERFORMANCE

Critic Stanley Kauffmann found Jack Nicholson's perfor-mance as McMurphy simply "tremendous": a revelation of the unhealthy reality within the "heroic" personality.

So Nicholson was ready for this film when the film was ready to be made. His very first scene as McMurphy jarred me. Re-leased from handcuffs after being transported from jail to hos-pital, he leaps and whoops for joy. It's coarsely, tritely done. But from then on he never sets a foot—an eyebrow—wrong. Walk-ing down the hall between attendants after that first scene, he is quite perceptibly playing a man who is an actor entering on a new stage, but he gives a quick look over his shoulder at a nurse who passes behind him—just a glance in passing—that also establishes him as a jungle animal on guard.

I'm not going to try to detail Nicholson's success through-out—from easy scenes (for him) like the horror of electric-shock treatment to subtler scenes like the welling of pleasure in him when he learns that the giant Indian is not really deaf and dumb and has duped the doctors. All of it creates a human being—a man who doesn't want to be anything but a star in *life*, who can't abide anything but control and attention, who wants the power to dispense favors and justice and, since he does little in life to justify that power, runs into areas of delu-sion, of frustration, of consequent violence. The film as a whole is warped, sentimental, possibly dangerous; but Nicholson is tremendous.

Stanley Kauffmann, "Jack High," *New Republic*, 13 December 1975: 22–23.

vulnerable Billy Bibbit, Will Sampson as the stolid, totem-like Chief Bromden. . . . They have been cast and assembled and directed with an eye for the visually expressive, the wayward, the comic, the pathetic.

The film has the unexpectedly buoyant feeling of a comic ballet of beautifully balanced mixed moods. It is only when we are forced to confront the message that it becomes ordinary, for it all boils down to yet another tug-o-war between the "ins" (the hip, the fun people) and the "outs" (the ogres, the squares): a child's view of the universe.

But Forman, coming from Czechoslovakia and having seen more than he would like to of institutional tyranny, is coming at "Cuckoo's Nest" from a cultural angle that entitles him to a more dialectical view of society.

FORMAN DEFENDS HIS USE OF THE INSANE AS CHARACTERS

"Why shouldn't insane people seem more appealing," he said in answer to my question, "Aren't we more interesting and more appealing than our government officials? Everybody who involves himself with oppressive machinery is paying for it with a loss of humor, with grayness.

"And don't forget," he added, "this is a ward of only moderately crazy people. The hopeless ones are upstairs." (They are enacted by real patients, and we see them whenever one of the characters goes up for shock treatment.)

We talked about the incredible faces, sad and wistful, of the actors who play the main characters. "You know, I never saw a handsome person institutionalized," Forman said. "The loss of self-respect is what causes mental disturbance. Somebody who can't find any way to build self-respect is very vulnerable to mental disease."

Forman said the shooting of the film at the Oregon State Hospital had had a therapeutic effect on the patients. "They're always trying to give patients the feeling that they're accomplishing something . . . but how can you feel this if you're mopping the floor from morning to night? With this film, they got very excited, they all said 'Oh, boy, we're making a Hollywood film.' It sounds like a cliche, but one man who hadn't opened his mouth for years left the institution two weeks after the film was made, talking.

"Sometimes we forget," Forman continued, "what a change has taken place in our view of mental illness. Institutions used to be created to protect the community from

Evil! This one was built in 1883, at which time it was five miles from the nearest house. Today it's in the middle of the city. We have to live with the insane, so we had better accept them as human beings."

DISTANCING THE FILM FROM '60S PSYCHEDELIA

I asked him about his decision, implemented in the screenplay of Lawrence Hauben and Bo Goldman, to treat the story objectively rather than through the eyes of the Indian, Kesey's point-of-view character.

"I didn't want that for my movie," he said. "I hate that voice-over, I hate that whole psychedelic '60s drug free-association thing, going with the camera through somebody's head. That's fine in the book, or on a stage, which is stylized. But in film the sky is real, the grass is real, the tree is real; the people had better be real too.

"You know, I'm glad I didn't know the reputation of the book when I read it, so I didn't have this artificial reverence for the 'cult classic.' And I think it's much better that it was made now than in the '60s. After a certain time, all the distracting elements fall away, all the transitory psychedelic stuff. And we can follow what it is really about. My film is very simple."

DANGEROUS CONVICTIONS

I told him I had certain reservations about the ending, particularly the diabolical revenge of the nurse which takes an even more extreme form than in the novel.

"She is dangerous," said Forman, "because she really believes what she is doing. I have seen this situation, and I know that authority in trouble will sacrifice anything and anyone to prove its point."

The Camera as Narrator

Thomas J. Slater

Minor differences exist between the novel and the film *One Flew Over the Cuckoo's Nest,* according to Thomas J. Slater, author of *Milos Forman: A Bio-Bibliography.* One of these is the fact that only the Chief is freed at the end of the film, which reflects his newfound courage (as opposed to the continuing cowardice of the other inmates). Another is that the power struggle taking place in the film is not between the Combine and everyone else, but between individuals. Also, both McMurphy and Nurse Ratched are nowhere nearly so clearly defined in the film as they are in the novel. Instead of the distinct good versus evil characters of the book, they become infinitely more complex, hazy, and ambivalent. The movie robs McMurphy of his unambiguous savior-hero role, making him partly responsible for his own demise; at the same time, it gives the Nurse a more humane and professional (though still misguided) quality. And finally, there is a difference in point of view between the novel's use of Chief Bromden as narrator and the film's use of the camera in this role. These differences, writes Slater, reflect director Milos Forman's themes more than Kesey's.

However, Forman "remains true to the spirit of Kesey's novel," says Slater. These differences were created mainly to update the '60s sensibility of the novel and give the film more currency. But Slater claims that rather than completely abandoning the Chief's perspective, Forman has instead added to it. In a novel written in the first person, readers get one point of view; in a movie that makes use of expert camera shots and angles, that point of view is more all-seeing and expanded.

Excerpted from Thomas J. Slater, "*One Flew Over the Cuckoo's Nest:* A Tale of Two Decades," in *Film and Literature: A Comparative Approach to Adaptation,* edited by Wendell Aycock and Michael Schoenecke (Lubbock: Texas Tech University Press, 1968). Reprinted by permission of the publisher.

When adapting Ken Kesey's *One Flew Over the Cuckoo's Nest* for the screen, Milos Forman faced one very significant problem: the novel's narrator is a paranoid-schizophrenic who sees things that nobody else can. Seen through the eyes of the six-foot-eight American Indian named Chief Bromden, *Cuckoo's Nest's* main setting of a mental ward at the Oregon State Hospital becomes a surrealistic world controlled by hidden wires and fog machines that help the head nurse and her staff to work their will on the patients. Although the Chief's vision is comic and absurd, it also reveals the reality of the world and the events that take place. As he accurately notes, "It's the truth, even if it didn't happen."

Forman also faced the problem of making Kesey's liberal early-sixties' theme of fighting conformity relevant to the mid-seventies. Forman had to make the story contemporary without losing its essence. He was successful mainly because he gave the novel's unusual narrative perspective to his camera and transformed Kesey's mythic characters and surrealist setting into human beings in a unique but recognizable world. . . .

RELEVANCE FIFTEEN YEARS LATER

Milos Forman remains true to the spirit of Kesey's novel by keeping his basic message but renovating the story to make it relevant to the mid-seventies. In the film, Forman's camera appropriately takes over the narrative perspective of both the Chief and Ken Kesey. Like the Chief in the novel, the camera presents McMurphy as a mythic figure while, at the same time, undercutting that notion. In the end, the viewer must realize his own responsibility for going beyond the philosophies of both McMurphy and Nurse Ratched. Once again, the Chief provides the final example to be followed.

In contrast to the book, the movie establishes the Chief as the only character that McMurphy sets free because he is the only one who has gained the courage to act on his own. Forman gives the story a contemporary meaning by showing it as a struggle for power among McMurphy, Ratched, and Harding. On its surface, Forman's film appears to have a conservative message because the hero is battling an oppressive social system dominated by a woman and a homosexual (Dale Harding), but his film is neither sexist nor anti-gay. His depiction of all three characters as failing to achieve or maintain power because of their very lust for it presents his true theme. Forman shows that people who strive for power are susceptible to their own human weaknesses, a fact that everyone needs to realize. In the end, each individual must work towards his or her own freedom or remain entrapped by the whims of those in power.

CAMERA SHOTS PROVIDE PERSPECTIVE

Forman begins by translating the Chief's characterization of McMurphy as a mythic hero onto the screen. The opening shot shows the red light of daybreak glowing out over a dark mountain. The music starts with the sound of an American Indian drumbeat, which is joined by a gentle folk guitar and a mournful harmonica that also has a mocking tone to it, like something has passed but does not really merit deep sympathy. Emerging from the deep shadows of the mountain are the headlights of the police car bringing McMurphy from the prison camp to the hospital.

In this one shot, Forman creates McMurphy as a mythic figure. McMurphy represents the freedom and elemental forces associated with the American wilderness. The mountain becomes an important symbol of manhood. When the Chief is ready to leave the hospital at the end of the film, he tells the comatose McMurphy that he is "big as a damn mountain." The native and folk music associates McMurphy with the basic instincts of Americans who are closely related to the land and do not have much power, people such as American Indians, farmers, and mountain people. The harmonica sounds like a lament, but McMurphy is not a character who would mourn anything and so the slightly mocking tone is appropriate. When the Chief makes his escape at the end, the harmonica tune becomes a brief, joyously orchestrated crescendo before lapsing again into a gentle murmur. The music thus emphasizes Forman's theme that the human spirit can, at times, overcome despair and burst forth in triumph.

For the second shot of the film, Forman pans from a window inside the hospital ward across the bed of one of the patients and on through the room. The shot is from the viewpoint of a patient who could have been watching the car coming and then turned to look back across the room. Scattered patches of red light coming from the window break the darkness of the ward, like sunlight seen from under water. Forman maintains the association of the red light with freedom and the idea of the men being kept like fish in an aquarium throughout the entire film. The ward's red exit signs constantly beckon the men towards a different world, one whose uncertainty makes them reluctant to leave their safe confines, despite the abuse they suffer.[1]

Forman's starting the shot from the barrier formed between the two worlds by the wall and the opposite movement of the camera from the opening shot further support his quick division of the world in the film between the outside and the inside. This division does not exist in the novel, where the Combine operates everywhere. In the film, McMurphy enables the men to experience freedom and dignity by taking them away from the hospital by involving them in sports such as basketball and fishing. McMurphy starts simply, within the ward. When he arrives, four of the men, Charlie Cheswick (Sidney Lassick), Billy Bibbit (Brad Dourif), Harding (William Redfield), and Martini (Danny DeVito) are playing cards.[2] McMurphy gathers his first follower by flashing his own deck of pornographic playing cards at Martini and luring him away. This action demonstrates that McMurphy is presenting the men an alternative reality more appealing to them than anything they have experienced before. Forman, however, has already begun to undercut McMurphy. When the police first take the handcuffs off him, McMurphy begins jumping around and screeching like a monkey. The action is funny, but it also shows that an uncontrolled nature is not completely desirable. Society has good reasons for taming the forces with which McMurphy is associated. But, in the mental hospital, it has gone too far. The film, therefore, like the novel, must demonstrate that a middle path between the extremes of McMurphy and Ratched does exist.

THE CAMERA SEES A DIFFERENT MCMURPHY THAN HERO-SAVIOR OF NOVEL

McMurphy is also a Christ-figure in the film, but Forman suggests the idea much more subtly than the Chief does in the novel. He shows McMurphy on the ward for the first time exercising with the other men before the daily therapy

---

1. Stanley Kauffmann gives Forman particular credit for his control in these opening shots and also heaps praise on Nicholson. 2. Casting the patients was crucial to Forman: "Since [they] have few lines to say, [the] audience must remember each simply by their look" (Burke, "The Director's Approach," 15).

session. Forman shoots him from behind as McMurphy
stands briefly with his arms stretched out in the crucifix position. The camera angle is significant because it emphasizes that McMurphy is not conscious of others seeing him
as a Christ-figure. In the film, he never shows any intention
of playing the hero. He makes all of his challenges to Nurse
Ratched when he has no knowledge of her power to keep
him institutionalized indefinitely. He acts openly only because he does not understand the risk he is taking.

For example, during the scene in which McMurphy tries
teaching the Chief (Will Sampson) how to play basketball,
Forman demonstrates the enormity of his spirit in comparison with the other men. McMurphy climbs onto the shoul-
ders of another patient, Bancini. When Bancini begins to run
around, McMurphy starts screaming, "Hit me, Chief! I'm
open." His voice fills the soundtrack, giving the impression
that he is now the dominant force at the hospital, but Forman's camera is on Nurse Ratched, watching from an omnipotent position inside the hospital. She maintains the
power and McMurphy's optimism is false. Once again, Forman uses the perspective of another patient, this time one
who is standing on the sidelines, whose simple vision both
supports and undercuts McMurphy's lofty stature.

In the fishing trip sequence, Forman undercuts McMurphy through a combination of the camera's point of view
and an alteration in the narrative structure. In this scene,
Forman strongly emphasizes the idea that the men are taking on new identities. McMurphy manages to confiscate a
rental boat by telling the harbor manager that the men are
doctors from the mental hospital. Forman captures the men
in individual shots as McMurphy introduces them, and they
all look suddenly sophisticated.[3] McMurphy gets the men
started fishing and then goes below deck with his girlfriend.
Martini immediately leads the men up front to try to peek in
the windows. Chaos erupts when Cheswick turns around,
sees no one on deck, and leaves the steering wheel. The boat
starts going crazy, McMurphy comes up on deck, and Taber
(Christopher Lloyd) hooks a fish. All of the men struggle together to bring it in while Harding and Cheswick fight over
the steering wheel. Forman pulls up to a high shot to show

3. Michael Wood finds Forman's theme of individual responsibility clearly expressed
in the scene of the men boarding the boat.

the boat going in a circle, thus communicating one of the problems with McMurphy's influence. Though the men are feeling free, McMurphy is actually leading them in circles. They are merely bouncing from Nurse Ratched's control into his.

MORE OMNISCIENT THAN CHIEF, CAMERA EMPHASIZES DIFFERENT THEMES

In this shot, Forman copies the Chief's narrative perspective in the book exactly. The difference is that the Chief interprets what he sees in purely optimistic terms, whereas Forman's shot captures the full complexity of the situation. Although he is a part of the group, the Chief also imagines himself high above the men and sees their laughter crashing in waves on shores all over the world. In the film, the Chief is not even on the boat, a fact relevant not only to Forman's change of narrator, but also to his alteration of the story to emphasize his own distinct themes. In the novel, the fishing trip and the basketball game between the patients and the aides both take place after McMurphy has already learned about Nurse Ratched's power over him. Forman places both events before McMurphy's discovery of this fact. Thus, McMurphy is not taking a conscious risk in the film; he is acting out of a pure desire to prove himself to the men and have some pleasure, feeding his own ego and libido at the same time. Kesey makes the trip a major step in McMurphy's aid to the Chief's transformation, but Forman replaces the theme of spiritual growth with an examination of individuals in a struggle for power. The three characters who seek it, McMurphy, Ratched, and Harding, all fail, leaving each of the men ultimately responsible for facing the world on his own.

By showing that he never consciously plays a hero's role, Forman undercuts McMurphy's mythic image thoroughly. In the novel, when McMurphy smashes the glass in Nurse Ratched's office window, the Chief describes him as carefully contemplating his action beforehand. In the film, McMurphy acts out of anger while surrounded by chaos. Taber has been carried away screaming after being burned by a cigarette that became lodged in his pant cuff, and Cheswick is hollering to get his confiscated cigarettes back. McMurphy first tries to silence him, but then goes in frustration to smash the window.

Similarly, at the end of the novel, McMurphy simply chooses not to leave the ward, and the Chief once again allows for the possibility that McMurphy's act is a heroic gesture. Forman shows McMurphy as unable to leave; when the aides arrive in the morning, he is still passed out on the floor from the previous night's party. Forman's shot of him lying there summarizes his conception of the character. The empty liquor bottle next to him, its former contents a source of both liberation and entrapment, is a reflection of McMurphy himself. Without self-control, the spirits of both have been wasted.

When McMurphy finally attacks Nurse Ratched, he is again acting impulsively. Shortly before, he is about to escape when Billy Bibbit's body is discovered. McMurphy's girlfriends call from outside the open window, but he cannot keep himself from returning to the scene. Nurse Ratched attempts to reassert the old order and McMurphy, realizing that he is losing his power, attacks. Even if his action is interpreted as a sacrifice, his own lack of conscious behavior has created the entire situation in the first place. Ultimately, McMurphy has no one but himself to blame for his suffering.

NICHOLSON'S COMPLEX MCMURPHY

Jack Nicholson deserves much credit for creating McMurphy as a powerfully ambiguous character, both appealing and repulsive.[4] When he acts like a baboon upon entering the hospital, Nicholson indicates that McMurphy is a character who lives on his own level of existence. This factor is the source of both his power and his downfall; he fascinates everyone, but no one can figure him out. All the patients think he is crazy for acting as boldly as he does, but follow him as if he were sane. All the doctors, and Nurse Ratched, believe he is sane, but treat him as if he were crazy. Meanwhile, the audience must question who is really mentally ill, the patients or the staff. Nicholson illustrates the power in McMurphy's own brand of insanity in one key scene.

McMurphy's attempt to lift a shower control panel seems idiotic at first. He begins by taking some deep breaths, working himself into a frenzy, and uttering some gibberish as if he were speaking in tongues. As he strains to lift the panel,

4. Pauline Kael provides significant insights into Jack Nicholson's careful handling of the McMurphy role, showing how Nicholson created ambiguity while avoiding the temptation to flaunt his shrewdness.

every vein in his arms and neck seems to pop up. He is clearly entering his own distinct reality. When he fails and challenges the other patients for not even trying, he gains the admiration of his fellow patients. By contrast, Forman questions McMurphy's sanity most at a time that appears to be his peak. At the end of the party he creates on the ward, the night before he is supposed to leave, McMurphy sits down to wait while Billy Bibbit goes to make love to the prostitute, Candy (Maria Small). The ward is in chaos, and the men are all drunk. It is McMurphy's moment of triumph. He gazes around with a self-satisfied smirk on his face. The camera holds him in a long close-up, forcing the viewer to stop to consider the image deeply. McMurphy's destructiveness does not make him an admirable figure to follow.

If McMurphy's ideal world is one of complete disarray, Nurse Ratched's is one of total order. Forman reveals this aspect of her personality in his first shot of her entering the ward. She wears a black cape and hat that forms a perfect color balance between herself and the three black aides, who all wear starched white uniforms. Later, Forman uses red light, which indicated a new day dawning for the men in the opening shot of the film, to represent the entrance to what Nurse Ratched considers to be freedom. Significantly, the hallway of the ward is lined with jail cells filled with men probably considered to be hopeless cases. The dominant empty whiteness represents the blank future toward which the hospital methods are leading the men. In one shot, a bright rectangular white light shines at the end of the hall, an image of the future. In contrast with McMurphy, Nurse Ratched promises a future devoid of life and color; however, Forman never makes Nurse Ratched into a mythic figure. Instead, she is a very human character whose evil is greater than she realizes. She is as unconscious of her destructiveness as McMurphy is of his positive aspects.

Camera Blurs Villain and Hero

The combination of Forman's camera and Louise Fletcher's performance truly defines Nurse Ratched as a person whose initially good intentions have been transformed into oppressiveness.[5] Because she is not a character of mythic propor-

---

5. Aljean Harmetz explains the importance of Louise Fletcher's contributions.

tions, Nurse Ratched is never called Big Nurse in the film. She is even referred to by her first name, Mildred.

Forman presents Nurse Ratched as a character who genuinely believes that she has the patients' best interests at heart, and Louise Fletcher offers no hint that the situation might be otherwise. The most obvious example of her non-maliciousness occurs at the staff meeting when the doctors are trying to decide what they will do with McMurphy. When Nurse Ratched calmly states that they should not pass on their problem by sending him back to the prison farm, the camera is unable to capture a note of malice. Her statement that she thinks they can help him is made away from the camera and is dramatically ambiguous.

In this scene, Forman's camera once again correlates exactly with the Chief's perspective in the novel, and the film is again more complex because Nurse Ratched is seen as a human being. The Chief's view of her is clearly dehumanizing. He imagines her taking a sip of coffee and setting the cup smoldering from the heat of her lips. The novel then requires the reader to discern between the Chief's point of view and reality. Nevertheless, Bromden clearly presents Nurse Ratched as a mechanistic villain. In the film, Nurse Ratched does not blatantly overrule the other doctors' diagnosis as she does in the book. Instead, they ask for her opinion as a skilled professional. The viewer must ponder what is wrong about her judgment, which seems perfectly logical. The distinction between Nurse Ratched as the villain and McMurphy as the hero becomes significantly blurred.

Paradoxically, even though Forman's Nurse Ratched is more human, she is also more evil. In the novel, the Chief describes her as only the Combine's representative. In the film, there is no Combine. Nurse Ratched is the sole barrier between the men and the outside world, a fact that Forman strongly emphasizes when she returns to the ward in the morning after the party. She and the aides stand opposite the patients, forming a human wall between the men and the red exit sign beckoning them towards the outside. . . .

As indicated in the film's opening, McMurphy represents the unbridled freedom of the American wilderness. His opponent, Nurse Ratched, represents a highly structured and institutionalized social system, one that is concerned with men only as physical beings who need to perform as required without complaining. When the Chief throws the water control panel through a window at the end, he produces the unity of body and spirit for which McMurphy was striving. Hearing the crash, Taber wakes up and gives a triumphant yell; but he and the other men still remain inside the ward. Each of them, like each viewer, must take the first steps toward freedom on his own and be prepared to keep fighting to preserve it. *One Flew Over the Cuckoo's Nest* expresses many of Milos Forman's long-held beliefs about power and feelings of compassion for the people who lack it.[6] By capturing the spirit of Ken Kesey's novel while also giving its meaning a contemporary significance, Forman gained a popular audience and established himself as a prominent film adaptor of contemporary American works.

WORKS CITED

Buckley, Tom. 1981. "The Forman Formula." *New York Times Sunday Magazine* 1 March: 28, 31, 42–43, 50–53.

Burke, Tom. 1976. "The Director's Approach—Two Wives." *New York Times* 28 March 2:15.

Carroll, Peter N. 1982. *It Seemed Like Nothing Happened: The Tragedy and Promise of America in the 1970s.* New York: Holt, Rineheart, and Winston.

Forrey, Robert. 1975. "Ken Kesey's Psychopathic Savior: A Rejoinder." *Modern Fiction Studies* 21.2:222–30.

Harmetz, Aljean. 1975. "The Nurse Who Rules The 'Cuckoo's Nest.'" *New York Times* 30 Nov. 2:13.

Kael, Pauline. 1975. "The Bull Goose Loony." *New Yorker* 1 Dec.: 131–36.

Kauffmann, Stanley. 1975. "Jack High." *The New Republic* 13 Dec.: 22–23.

Kesey, Ken. 1962. *One Flew Over the Cuckoo's Nest.* New York: New American Library.

Muzzio, Douglas. 1982. *Watergate Games: Strategies, Choices, Outcomes.* New York: New York University Press.

6. Josef Skvorecky quotes Forman as saying, "I think all that which is noble, and which has remained in art and literature since ancient times . . . and which is also significant for strong contemporary works of art, has always concerned itself with injuries and injustices perpetrated against the individual. There, at the bottom of all those great works, are the injustices, which no social order will eliminate. Namely, that one is clever and the other is stupid, one is able and the other is incompetent, one is beautiful while the other is ugly, another might be honest, and yet another dishonest, and all of them are in some way ambitious. And it indeed does not matter that we are arriving at eternal themes."

Palumbo, Donald. 1983. "Kesey's and Forman's *One Flew Over the Cuckoo's Nest:* The Metamorphosis of Metamorphosis as Novel Becomes Film." *CEA Critic* 45.2:25–32.

Skvorecky, Josef. 1971. *All the Bright Young Men and Women: A Personal History of the Czech Cinema.* Toronto: Peter Martin Associates, Ltd.

Wallace, Ronald. 1979. *The Last Laugh: Form and Affirmation in the Contemporary American Comic Novel.* Columbia: University of Missouri Press.

Wood, Michael. 1976. "No. But I Read the Book." *New York Review of Books* 5 Feb.: 3–4.

Chronology

1960

Has first experiences with the mind-altering drug LSD as paid volunteer in government-sponsored scientific experiments; works as psychiatric aide in Menlo Park Veterans Administration mental hospital; daughter Shannon is born; John F. Kennedy is elected U.S. president.

AUGUST 1960–JUNE 1961

Writes first published novel, *One Flew Over the Cuckoo's Nest.*

1961

Son Zane is born.

1961–1963

Writes *Sometimes a Great Notion.*

1962

One Flew Over the Cuckoo's Nest is published.

1963

Moves to La Honda, California; son Jed is born; *One Flew Over the Cuckoo's Nest,* a stage play by Dale Wasserman and starring actor Kirk Douglas, opens on Broadway in New York; President Kennedy is assassinated.

1964

Sometimes a Great Notion is published; Merry Pranksters (Kesey and thirteen others) take cross-country trip from California to New York in wildly painted 1939 International Harvester school bus driven by Neal Cassady (real-life model for hero of Kerouac's *On the Road*).

1965

Merry Pranksters stage "Acid Tests," public LSD parties with psychedelic rock music and light shows; in first arrest for marijuana possession, Kesey is convicted but case is appealed.

1965–1973

Vietnam War.

1966

In second arrest for marijuana possession, Kesey flees to Mexico, where he remains for eight months; is arrested by FBI upon returning to the United States; daughter Sunshine is born in Mexico; LSD is declared an illegal substance by

U.S. government; stages public "Graduation from Acid."

1967

Serves five months in San Mateo County Jail and San Mateo County Sheriff's Honor Camp; young people flock to Haight-Ashbury in San Francisco as hippie and psychedelic culture spreads.

1968

Settles with his family in Pleasant Hill, Oregon; Neal Cassady dies; Tom Wolfe's *Electric Kool-Aid Acid Test* is published; Richard Nixon is elected U.S. president.

1969

Spends three months in England working for Apple Records on recording project involving writers' reading their works.

1970

Makes *Atlantis Rising,* an unreleased movie for children.

1971

Film of *Sometimes a Great Notion,* starring and directed by Paul Newman, is released (Kesey is not involved in project).

1973

Kesey's Garage Sale (miscellaneous writings between 1965 and 1973, which include drawings and comments on *Cuckoo's Nest*) is published.

1974

Nixon resigns U.S. presidency over Watergate scandal.

1974–1975

Travels in Egypt; writes about pyramids for *Rolling Stone* magazine.

1974–1981

Seven Prayers by Grandma Whittier (serialized novel) is published in Kesey's own publishing venture, called *Spit in the Ocean.*

1975

Film of *One Flew Over the Cuckoo's Nest,* starring Jack Nicholson and Louise Fletcher, is released (Kesey refuses to see it); wins five Oscar awards.

1978

Writes screenplay about Neal Cassady and Merry Prankster

bus (not published until 1990).

1979

Publishes "The Day After Superman Died," a tribute to Neal Cassady, in *Esquire* magazine.

1981

Publishes "Now We Know How Many Holes It Takes to Fill the Albert Hall: On the Passing of John Lennon" in *Rolling Stone.*

1981–1982

Covers Beijing Marathon in China for *Running* magazine.

1982

Visits Alaska; begins writing *Sailor Song.*

1984

Son Jed is killed in car accident en route to compete with the University of Oregon wrestling team.

1986

Demon Box (stories, essays, and journalism, 1973–1986) is published and dedicated to Jed; Kesey donates new high-quality team bus to the University of Oregon wrestling program.

1987–1988

Teaches creative writing at the University of Oregon at Eugene.

1989

Caverns (by O.U. Levon, a collaborative novel by Kesey and his University of Oregon creative writing class) is published.

1990

Little Tricker the Squirrel Meets Big Double the Bear is published; *The Furthur Inquiry* (a screenplay written in 1978 about Neal Cassady and the 1964 Merry Prankster bus trip) is published.

1991

The Sea Lion (children's story) is published.

1992

Sailor Song (novel) is published.

1993

Kesey goes on tour arranging festivals for amateur performers; gives readings of his books for children in full Native American dress at hospitals and schools.

1994

Last Go Round (Western tale), coauthored with Ken Babbs, is published.

1994–1995

Writes and performs *Twister* (unpublished play).

1997

Suffers mild stroke.

FOR FURTHER RESEARCH

WORKS BY KEN KESEY

One Flew Over the Cuckoo's Nest. New York: Viking, 1962. Novel.

Sometimes A Great Notion. New York: Viking, 1964. Novel.

Kesey's Garage Sale. New York: Viking, 1973. Stories, screenplay, nonfiction.

Seven Prayers by Grandma Whittier. In S*pit in the Ocean.* Pleasant Hill, Oregon: Intrepid Trips Information Service, 1974–1981. Serial novel.

Demon Box. New York: Viking, 1986. Stories, non-fiction.

Caverns (by O.U. Levon, a pen name for Kesey and his creative writing students). New York: Viking, 1989. Novel.

The Furthur Inquiry. New York: Viking, 1990. Screenplay.

Little Tricker the Squirrel Meets Big Double the Bear. New York: Viking Puffin, 1990. Children's story.

The Sea Lion. New York: Viking Puffin, 1991. Children's story.

Sailor Song. New York: Viking, 1992. Novel.

Last Go Round (with Ken Babbs). New York: Viking, 1994. Historical novel.

ABOUT KEN KESEY AND HIS WORKS

Bruce Carnes, *Ken Kesey.* Boise: Boise State University, 1974.

Barry Leeds, *Ken Kesey.* New York: Ungar, 1981.

Paul Perry and Ken Babbs, *On the Bus: The Complete Guide to the Legendary Trip of Ken Kesey and the Merry Pranksters and the Birth of the Counterculture.* New York: Thunder's Mouth, 1990.

M. Gilbert Porter, *The Art of Grit: Ken Kesey's Fiction.* Columbia: University of Missouri Press, 1982.

John Riley, "Bio: Novelist Ken Kesey Has Flown the 'Cuckoo's

Nest' and Given Up Tripping for Farming," *People*, March 22, 1976.

Michael Strelow, ed., "Kesey," *Northwest Review*, 1977.

Stephen L. Tanner, *Ken Kesey*. Boston: Twayne, 1983.

Tom Wolfe, *The Electric Kool-Aid Acid Test*. New York: Farrar, Straus & Giroux, 1968.

ABOUT *ONE FLEW OVER THE CUCKOO'S NEST*

John A. Barsness, "Ken Kesey: The Hero in Modern Dress," *Bulletin of the Rocky Mountain Language Association*, March 1969.

Peter G. Beidler and John W. Hunt, eds., "Perspectives on *Cuckoo's Nest:* A Symposium on Ken Kesey," *Lex et Scientia: The International Journal of Law and Science*, January–March 1977.

Thomas H. Fick, "The Hipster, the Hero, and the Psychic Frontier in *One Flew Over the Cuckoo's Nest*," *Rocky Mountain Review*, 1989.

Roger B. Henkle, "The Social Dynamics of Comedy," *Sewanee Review*, 1982.

Irving Malin, "Ken Kesey: *One Flew Over the Cuckoo's Nest*," *Critique*, 1962.

M. Gilbert Porter, One Flew Over the Cuckoo's Nest: *Rising to Heroism*. Boston: Twayne, 1989.

John Clark Pratt, ed., One Flew Over the Cuckoo's Nest: *Text and Criticism*. 1973. Reprint, New York: Viking Press, 1996.

Nathan A. Scott Jr., "History, Hope, and Literature," *Boundary*, 1973.

George J. Searles, ed., *A Casebook on Ken Kesey's* One Flew Over the Cuckoo's Nest. Albuquerque: University of New Mexico Press, 1992.

Stephen A. Shapiro, "The Ambivalent Animal: Man in the Contemporary British and American Novel," *Centennial Review*, 1968.

Wallace Stegner, "History, Myth, and the Western Writer," *American West*, 1967.

James M. Vardaman Jr., "Invisible Indian: Chief Bromden of Ken Kesey's *One Flew Over the Cuckoo's Nest*," *Journal English Institute*, 1980.

Rene Wellek, "The Attack on Literature," *American Scholar,* Winter 1972–1973.

Gary A. Wiener, "From Huck to Holden to Bromden: The Non-Conformist in *One Flew Over the Cuckoo's Nest,*" *Studies in the Humanities,* 1979.

Michael P. Woolf, "The Madman as Hero in Contemporary American Fiction," *Journal of American Studies,* 1976.

WEBSITES

Intrepid Trips (www.IntrepidTrips.com). A website with links to many other Kesey-related sites.

Kesey Bibliography (www.charm.net/~Brooklyn/Biblio/KeseyBiblio.html). A detailed listing of his works, performance art, books read by him on tape, film, videos, lectures, letters, LPs, interviews, and more.

K-Z Productions (www.key-z.com). Created by Kesey's son Zane, this site includes interesting information on Kesey and the Merry Pranksters.

1998 Roster (www.clark.net/pub/cosmic/98pbr.html). Features many images of "Prankster Busriders" and information on Kesey, Jack Kerouac, Neal Cassady, and others of their era.

INDEX